# What's Wrong With Me?

## Breaking the Chain
## of
## Adolescent Codependency

# Lonny Owen

DEACONESS PRESS

# What's Wrong With Me?

## Breaking the Chain
## of
## Adolescent Codependency

Lonny Owen

# Contents

## Dedication

This book is dedicated to my daughter Rachelle (Shelly) and my son Jerehmy. My love for both of you is why this book was written. I also dedicate this book to myself.

# Acknowledgements

This book could not have been written without the presence of certain people in my life.

First of all, my parents. They passed on to me the gift of perseverance which, as a young person, I mistook for "bullheaded-ness." Without their gift, I could not have stuck in there to complete my work.

Next are my close A.A friends who were consistently telling me to "hang in there" just when I needed to hear it.

Then come the authors of recovery books dealing with code-pendency. Without their pioneering work dealing with this difficult and sometimes controversial subject, I could not have possibly completed my work. These authors include Sharon Weigschieder-Cruise, Earnie Larson, Sondra Smalley, Claudia Black, Robert Subby, John Bradshaw, Louie Anderson, and Melody Beattie.

I am very fortunate to know Melody Beattie as a friend. Besides her inspirational writing which has helped in my personal recovery, Melody has become a role model for me as a writer. When I became confused and fearful, she offered me insight and courage. When I was tired, she gave me energy by telling me she believed in me. And most importantly, she told me what I needed to hear rather than what I may have wanted to hear. Thanks, Melody.

Finally, there are my personal friends who have put up with me through this process. One special friend, Darlene Kari, has always been there giving me constant nurturing and reassurance no matter how crazy things got.

Thank you all. You are the reason I was able to complete this book.

# *Introduction*

This book is for everyone concerned with the numerous problems affecting young people today, problems like chemical dependency, eating disorders, depression, suicide, criminal behavior, sexual acting out, teenage pregnancy, and gambling. There are many more.

This book is for parents, brothers and sisters, concerned friends, teachers, helping professionals, probation officers, police officers, lawyers, and judges—anyone who has a major impact on the lives of young people. But most importantly, it's for the young person trying to understand how to deal with these problems.

This book took a long time to come about. As a recovering alcoholic of fourteen years and a chemical dependency counselor of eleven years, I had always suspected there was something missing when it came to helping chemically dependent youth. At first, I thought we needed to confront their parents. You see, in my work counseling young people, I would meet these parents and discover they were either active or recovering alcoholics, drug addicts, or appeared to have some sort of stress-related problem. This, I thought, made them inadequate parents—so it was *their* fault their kids were so messed up!

Only until six years ago did I discover how wrong I had been. About this time, I hit some kind of emotional bottom. I was out of work and depressed, and searching for answers to what was happening to me. I found many of these answers after reading several books about codependency and adult children of alcoholics. I discovered that there were many things that had happened in my early life that was continuing to affect me in painful ways. I gained an understanding as to how my alcoholism was brought about as a way of surviving childhood abuse and neglect. I still understand my need to deal with my alcoholism as a primary problem. But to be truly happy—free of chronic emotional pain—I needed to enter into a process of recovery from my codependency. This would also help me prevent relapse into my old addiction and head-off acquiring new ones like gambling, work, and sex.

The major part of this process for me was to do what was called *Family of Origin* work. By doing this, I learned many things— especially about my parents. And that was this:

### It wasn't their fault.

For years, I had suffered with feelings of rejection and unworthiness. I felt anger and rage towards my parents. But my parents were only passing on what was passed on to them. My father had been raised and then deserted by an alcoholic father at age fifteen. Knowing this, I saw my father for the first time in a different light. I felt compassion and love for him. I saw that innocent fifteen-year-old who had lost his father and thus the ability to learn how to *be* a father. I began to give him credit for trying the best he could. That's why I don't blame parents anymore. We're *not* to blame. Nobody is.

Did you notice I said *we?* I'm one of those parents I used to blame. I, too, passed on to my children what was passed on to me. I used to feel extremely guilty about this, but no more. I am dealing with my codependency, and I'm passing my *recovery* on to my children. I do this by talking to my children about what I have learned about my family, and by encouraging their questions. This book was written as a tool for you to do the same. It explains to young people how families operate. It helps them figure out how their family is operating. It offers insight as to how young people may be reacting to other messages they get from society and their peers that aren't serving them well. This book concludes with information about what they can do to help themselves through involvement in recovery programs.

Although I knew a good deal about this subject before writing this book, I learned even more after its completion. I suspect the same will happen to you once you read the book. You see, I had to write it from the perspective of a sixteen-year-old. I suggest you read it in the same manner. Then pass it on to your child or a young person you are concerned about. You will be passing on information that offers hope for recovery—recovery for our children.

*What's Wrong With Me?*

## Chapter One

# *What Is Codependency and Why Should I Learn About It?*

Codependency is the hidden cause that sets us up for major problems like chemical dependency, eating disorders, depression, and criminal behavior. If you are having any of these problems, or are living with people with such problems, codependency is probably behind it. Adults have been learning about how to understand and deal with their codependency. Now it's your turn.

There is no right way to define codependency—especially adolescent codependency. It is made up of many different parts. I am going to give you a broad definition, and then discuss these various parts. You decide if it fits in to any problems you may be having. Here goes:

> *Adolescent codependency is emotional stress, confusion, fear and pain brought on by events in our*

1

> *family and society which messes up our healthy*
> *development into adulthood. Our reaction is to take*
> *on one or more survival behaviors. These behaviors,*
> *together with the events that set them up, are passed*
> *on from generation to generation through our*
> *families and society.*

*Survival* is the key word. We attempt to survive things like neglect, physical abuse, sexual abuse, parental alcoholism and drug addiction, and abandonment. It's OK to survive. It's OK to do what we need to survive. But some of these behaviors we learn can become just as destructive as the problems we are trying to survive— problems like alcohol and drug abuse.

Let's say we are living in an alcoholic family. We swear we'll never drink as much or do things our alcoholic parent is doing. The next thing we know, we're busted for things like minor consumption, or we're kicked out of school for possession of drugs. Eventually, we could become as addicted to alcohol or drugs as our alcoholic parent. Again, we are not to be blamed for this. Nor should we blame ourselves. Yet we are stuck with having to deal with another major problem. It's an example of how families pass on their problems to us. We'll learn more about how and why this happens as we read on.

There are ways to get out of a bind like this. It begins with awareness—awareness of what makes us click, and learning about why we keep doing things that are hurting us even when we want to change them. It also means learning about how families operate, the roles we play in our family and why, and figuring out the messages we receive from our family and society which make up the rules we follow. Finally, to get out of the bind, we need to learn about *affirmations* (positive statements we give ourselves to fight the shame we may have picked up from messed up messages our

2

parents, society, and peers gave us). This is what understanding our codependency is all about.

Understanding our codependency ends with learning about recovery. We learn that we are not alone in our struggle. Though we are young, we can figure out all our problems and make healthy decisions about how to handle them. We can learn that there are people who care about us, and we can learn to care about ourselves. We discover that we can be happy regardless of our situation.

## Suggested Activity:

Throughout the book, I will end each chapter with a suggested activity or activities based on the information in that chapter. This will help process (figure out) how this information applies to us. Don't think at this point that you should understand what codependency is all about. We're just getting started. It will add up as we go on.

## Chapter Two

# *How Families Operate*

Our first step is to learn how families operate. A family is where we get our food and shelter. A family gives us safety from things that might hurt us, and gives us love and a sense of feeling important. A family is where we can ask questions and get answers when we are confused.

The parents or parent in our families are healthy people who we look up to. We want to be like them. Our parents help us learn by giving us fair consequences when we mess up. They focus on our behavior and never put us down, reject, or abandon us. They realize as teenagers that we need a little more room to operate, to experiment a little. They give us this room. Our parents give us encouragement to pursue our dreams, no matter what they are.

They never force us into being what they think we should be. Finally, we're all close to our brothers and sisters with whom we can share anything.

As you were reading this, did you think to yourself, "This isn't my family." Me, too. In fact, my family operates almost the opposite.

What I was describing is the perfect family. There are very few, if any, perfect families around. Most of us are in not-so-perfect families. This was important for me to learn because, as a young person, I thought I was the only one who had a not-so-perfect family. I didn't talk to my friends about it because this would make me feel weird—not like them. I was ashamed of my family and ashamed of myself. I felt odd. Different. Defective. I didn't think I fit in anywhere.

I don't feel this way anymore. I've learned about how families operate—especially my family. I've learned how my parents were passing on their experiences as children to me. Their experiences, I discovered, weren't that perfect either.

To understand this more, we need to learn how families operate as a system, how we develop and play roles in our family, how we pick up messages from our family, and how families hold on to secrets. Finally, we need to learn how all of this is passed on from generation to generation through our family tree.

## Families Are Systems

This means that all family members are emotionally hooked up or connected to one another. What family members say and do affects us even if these things aren't said or done to us. If mom and

6

dad are fighting and we're in our room listening, we might be affected by fearing that they might get a divorce—or even abandon us. We might even feel responsible for their fighting. Perhaps we have a brother or sister who is abusing alcohol or drugs and our parents start looking through our room for drugs. We might feel mistrusted and angry that our privacy has been invaded. In both of these situations, we may not have done anything. But we were affected because we are in a *family system*. These feelings also produce *stress*. Now we have to figure out how to deal with it.

Another way to describe how a family works as a system is to compare it to a machine—a machine like a bicycle. For a bike to work smoothly, the chain has to be firmly on the pedal sprocket and the rear wheel sprocket. The tires need to be fastened firmly onto the frame and full of air. Now all you need is a responsible rider who takes good care of the bike and everything runs smoothly.

Family systems work the same way. If everyone in the family is hooked up right and working together like the parts of the bike, and we have a responsible rider (our parents), things run pretty smoothly.

Now lets think about how well this bike would operate if the rider was an alcoholic. Do you think this bike would be well looked after? It would probably be pretty banged up—and eventually wrecked. That's exactly what happens when our family system is driven by something stressful like alcoholism.

## Family Roles

Have you ever heard the term *Black Sheep of the Family*? How about *Jock, Clown, Rebel,* or *Burnout*? Most of us have heard at

least one of these terms used. They are words that describe *roles*—
roles we learn to play in our family. We are appointed these roles.
We don't ask for them. All families operate this way. What role or
roles we learn to play depends on what the family needs for it to
operate or *function.*

In her book *The Family Trap*, Sharon Wegscheider describes
five typical roles played by members of chemically dependent
families. All families develop these roles to a certain extent. All
families experience some degree of stress. The amount of stress
then reflects how rigid these roles are. These roles aren't all bad.
We will all play one or more of them over the course of a lifetime.
A brief discussion of these five roles follows.

## The Enabler

The *enabler* is usually the wife or husband of a chemically
dependent parent. This person is said to enable or allow the
alcoholic or drug addict to continue using. The enabler does this by
developing caretaking behaviors such as picking up after the
chemically dependent person after they get high or drunk, or calling
in to work for this chemically dependent person saying they are
"sick" when they are actually hung over. This then allows the
chemically dependent person to escape the consequences of drinking or drug abuse. The enabler also attempts to control the drinking
or drug abuse by doing things like pouring alcohol down the drain,
or throwing drugs away. The enabler does these things thinking that
they may help the addicted person stop using or drinking.

The enabler has a hard time admitting that they cannot control
an abuser's behavior. They try many things to change the abuser.

They think it will get better. They think: "If only I just do..." All this takes a great deal of time and emotional energy—and nothing ever seems to work right. With all this time spent on trying to change the chemically dependent person in the family, there isn't much time left for the rest of the family members. Maybe you can relate to this if you are from a chemically dependent family. You may be just as angry at the non-addicted parent as the addicted one. Perhaps both parents have alcohol or drug problems, and you have an older brother or sister who plays the enabler role. You may even play it yourself.

What we are beginning to talk about now is *denial*—denial that the problem is bad, and thinking we can change it. We deny even to our friends when they suggest that maybe our parents or a brother or sister has a problem with alcohol or drugs. Then it becomes a *family secret*. There are many of these family secrets. I will talk more about them in the next section.

Whether they be a husband or wife of a chemically dependent person, or a brother or sister—or even ourselves—an enabler is *not to be blamed*. An enabler is only trying to survive. The enabler is *not* responsible for an abuser's problem. For a chemically dependent family to operate—although in a crazy way—it needs at least one enabler.

## Family Hero

The family hero is usually the firstborn child in the family. Up to this point, the family was only a husband and wife. Now they have a child which makes them a real family. This means that, automatically, a lot is expected of this child. They have to "do the family

9

proud." This puts a lot of pressure on them to succeed in all they do throughout their life. That makes it very hard for the hero to fail at anything. Typically, a family hero:

- looks good.
- does what's right.
- gets good grades.
- has lots of friends.
- does great in sports.
- is never wrong.
- always wins.

We may be very angry at the family hero because they seem to get the most recognition from our parents.

Here's the problem for the hero: inside, they feel terribly inadequate because, at times, they will fail. Nobody is perfect, and nobody can possibly reach perfection in all that they do. So whenever they fail, the hero feels even more inadequate. They may begin to fear failure so much that they set themselves up to fail early in order to reduce the fear. Some will take shortcuts to success, like using steroids to improve their performance in sports, or—to deal with stress—use alcohol more than the "heavier " drugs because they think it is more acceptable.

The hero may also find that acting out in any way is too much risk, and choose to *internalize* or stuff the stressful feelings. This may cause depression or a number of stress-related health problems. I've noticed that many heroes go through their life always feeling sick, going to doctor after doctor trying to find out what is wrong. If the hero is fortunate enough to go to a doctor who understands that stress-related physical problems begin in stressful family systems, they may be referred to a therapist who can help. Unfortunately, this usually isn't the case, and the hero keeps striving to always be on top. They may become a workaholic, marry a chemically dependent person and become the adult enabler we discussed earlier, or die at a young age from a physical problem such as a heart attack. Many of us are surprised when someone who seems to have it all commits suicide. Many of these people are family heroes. The pressure of being on top and believing they need to do even more is too much for them. The sad part is, it doesn't have to be this way. Nor does it have to go this far. Awareness early in the hero's life, along with a desire to follow a recovery program, can result in a happy and fulfilling life. This is also true for the enabler and other people stuck in the roles we will talk about next.

## Scapegoat

So now we have a family with a chemically dependent adult, a husband or wife who doesn't know how to confront the problem so attempts to control it, and a child who diverts attention away from the problem by being perfect and making the family proud. Eventually, the chemical dependency problem in the family is at risk of being exposed without something or someone to blame. The enabler can always take on some of this, but they will eventually get wise and begin to confront the chemical dependency.

Along comes the *scapegoat*, usually the secondborn, who's appointed the job of taking the focus off the chemical dependency or other stressful problems in the family. We do this by becoming the problem in the family. I know about this role because I have been acting it out most of my life. Neither one of my parents are alcohol or drug dependent, but I believe my dad's father was. My dad has never accepted this and continues in denial. As a result, he has— without realizing it—passed on to his present family the stress from being in an alcoholic family. This is an example of how problems are passed on from one generation to another if it is held as a *family secret*. I'll talk later about how and why this happens.

Besides being a scapegoat, I've been called a rebel, radical, troublemaker, juvenile delinquent, and other assorted names I can't mention. These names didn't come by accident. I pretty much acted them out. When you've been told all your life you are a problem, you begin to believe it. I thought, "What the hell. If they say I'm all these things, I might as well *be* all these things." And I was. I made this decision around the age of twelve, the beginning of my teenage years.

Up till then, I had been trying to fight the idea that I was a problem with some help from a couple of caring school teachers who kept saying, "You're OK." They tried their best to give me confidence, but eventually my family—including an abusive grandmother and another relative—won out. I finally began acting out the scapegoat role with gusto. It felt safe and comfortable. Although I had begun drinking alcohol at around the age of eight (sneaking it from my dad's peppermint schnapps bottle), I now looked for every opportunity to party. I went to beer parties with my older sister. I offered to help my cousin baby-sit so I could get into the liquor cabinet at whatever place she was baby-sitting. I continued to sneak booze from the open bottles in our house and, at age fifteen—Utopia!—I joined a local rock & roll band. The good times didn't last long. By the time I was sixteen, I had been arrested and put on probation, had a couple of stays in the hospital for stitches, and was more or less living on my own as a result of several arguments with my parents. I continued drinking and using drugs for several years before finally getting help. I admitted that the booze and drugs got the best of me. I was chemically dependent.

So goes the life of many scapegoats. Behind all the hostility, defiance, and anger is a little boy or girl who is hurt and sad, looking for the love of their parents. Too many of us try to fill this emptiness with alcohol and drugs. But the drugs also let us down. Some of us get into crime and spend years of our young lives in jails or some kind of residential program. We become parents of children when we are still children ourselves—which robs us of what is supposed to be the best years of our lives.

I wish there would have been some way of understanding what was happening when, at the age of sixteen, I ran screaming down the street after a fight with my dad. I remember this as though it happened yesterday. I remember thinking: "Someone please tell me *what's wrong with me* so I can fix it!" If you have ever had the same type of thoughts, you've been heard. You've suffered enough. You are ready to begin your recovery. The first step is awareness. You are becoming more aware as you read on. Hang in there. Reading through this stuff can be an emotional trip. If you need to, put the book down. Come back to it later. If you are fortunate enough to have a parent, brother, sister or friend in a recovery program, talk to them about what you are thinking or feeling. This is called *taking care of yourself.*

## The Lost Child

Now we have a family with a *chemically dependent* parent, a parent who *enables,* a child *hero* the parents can be proud of, and a *scapegoat* to really stir things up. It's time for relief. That's what the *lost child's* role is.

A lost child is to be seen, not heard. Most of the time, they aren't even seen. They spend a lot of time in their room, reading, eating, or sleeping. I've noticed that lost children often develop eating disorders like obesity, anorexia, or bulimia. This is their way of surviving the stress of the problem in the family. Besides, with a hero and a scapegoat, there isn't much chance to get attention.

The lost child is left feeling lonely and unimportant. They are at risk of depression and suicidal thinking. They have few friends. They also have a hard time making decisions and are low on energy, not wanting to do much of anything. Because of their low self-esteem, they are followers and can be lead into almost anything. You might know a lost child. They are the ones who get teased a lot at school for being nerds or geeks. It might be the chubby girl who will put out to get accepted into the "in crowd." When they walk, their heads seem to hang down, showing how unimportant they feel. It's truly a sad and lonely existence.

The good news is that lost children in recovery can and do become independent, talented, creative, imaginative, and happy people. I have a sister who was a lost child. She struggled, but finally came out of her room. She is the most loving, caring, brightest, and happiest person in the family. She has found this in recovery. So can you.

## The Mascot

So far, we have a parent with a *chemical dependency* or other problem, an *enabler* working hard to change the problem, a *hero* to focus on and be proud of, a *scapegoat* to blame and who is acting out to get some attention, and a *lost child* who looks at all this and says, "To hell with it, I'm going to my room." What's left?

How about someone to lighten things up? That's the job of the *mascot*. They're the comic or clown in the family. The mascot learns this role at a very young age. They're the ones who come into the room when everyone is arguing and does something funny like stand on their head. The mascot learns that to get attention in the family, they must entertain everyone. They think: "It's important to make my family feel happy." They also feel responsible for the welfare of the family as a whole. A mascot might try to get the family together for family events. When they get older, they inform all their brothers and sisters of the parents' birthdays and anniversaries.

You all know a mascot. They're the funny ones at school. They seem to be happy and have a lot of friends—but they always feel they have to entertain them to be accepted. As a teenager, I had a good friend who was a mascot. He was accepted into the group because he would do anything we asked him to do. One time we promised him a case of beer if he would climb to the top of a flagpole on the main street of our town in the middle of the day—with his pants down.

He got his case of beer.

The mascot is very fearful of rejection. They tend to be hyperactive in school and very lonely. The friends they have are never really close. My only brother is the mascot in my family. He always has a new joke to tell. He is also a musician.

I've noticed that mascots who have worked on their problems make great comedians and entertainers. There probably wouldn't be much to watch on TV or at the movies without them.

## More About Roles

These roles don't always develop in the order I've described. It depends more on what the family needs at the time. Perhaps the problem between mom and dad is so intense that the firstborn needs to be the scapegoat so there is someone to blame.

Also, these roles may overlap. You may play part hero and part scapegoat at the same time. If you are an only child, you may play a number of roles—possibly all of them—at some time.

We play roles for two basic reasons: to get attention (love and nurturing), and to keep the family in balance and operating in some way. Even if the family is operating in a crazy way, it's what everybody is used to. It feels normal. And what's normal for a family under stress is to protect the *secret*—the real cause of the stress. This all sounds crazy—and it is.

Before we go on to *family secrets,* we need to discuss *role reversal.* This is when one of the children in the family takes on the role of parent. Role reversal can happen because of two situations arising in the family. First, it can happen when one of our parents becomes absent through divorce or death. If we're from a divorced family, we are either with our mother or father. We may visit the other parent, but we primarily live with one or the other. This leaves a hole in the family. It means the family doesn't operate very well without all its parts, just like the bicycle. If it's the father who is absent, the oldest son may become the man of the house. The oldest may lose out on the fun of being a teenager because they have to be grown up and responsible. If the mother is absent, the same thing can happen to the oldest girl. She will have to look after the kids, do the housework, and cook the meals. This robs us of our teenage years. We could become in our parent's eyes their mate—even become sexual with them.

This is a form of sexual abuse called *incest.* The parent is very confused and needs help. The victim of incest is likewise confused and feels ashamed. We'll talk more about incest in the section on *family secrets.*

A second type of situation that brings on role reversal is when we have both our parents, but one or both are not doing their parenting job very well. When this happens, one of the children takes over. Much of the time, it is the oldest—the hero. In my situation, my youngest sister took on the role of being the parent for my parents. It happened this way: Since the family needed a hero because most of us had moved, my youngest sister became the second hero in the family. She did very well in school (National Honor Society) and worked to buy herself a car and clothes. She also had a lot of friends.

One day, my sister brought a girlfriend to the house. The house was a disaster. This wasn't unusual because my parents have always had an unkept house. My sister was so angry and embarrassed, she had a talk with my parents after her friend had left. She told my parents that she was taking over—that she would run the house. And she did. She was fourteen years old at the time.

From that time on, my sister made sure all the dishes and the laundry was done. I remember my parents complaining how my sister was always telling them what to do—complaining just as a child might complain. Being a parent at fourteen has its consequences. Instead of pursuing her dreams and realizing her potential, my sister chose early marriage.

It's important to realize that these roles are about our behavior. They are not who we are. We all play roles. It's how families work. We don't have to suffer problems from these roles if we learn what to watch out for. That's what we are doing in this book—learning. We are learning about how families operate. We're learning about how *our* families operate. We will learn even more in the *Recovery* chapter of this book about how we can't do much about changing our family. But there is a great deal we can do to help change ourselves. We learn that there is a way out even if we have to continue living in a not-so-perfect family, a way out of being so effected by other people's problems. We learn how we may have developed or are developing a problem as a reaction to someone else's problem. We learn how unfair this is, and how we were set up to have this problem. We also learn that we can truly be happy, and free from pain through recovery.

Finally, these roles protect *family secrets*. Our next step is to learn more about them.

## Suggested Activity:

•List the role(s) you see yourself playing most often.

_____

_____

_____

_____

_____

_____

_____

_____

_____

_____

_____

_____

## Chapter Three

# *Family Secrets*

I've referred to *family secrets* a number of times. So what are they? You may have guessed already that they are a problem or problems that no one wants or knows how to deal with. You may also have figured out that these problems can be passed on to us if our parents don't bring them out into the open and deal with them. All families have unfortunate situations happen from time to time. Some of these families deal with these situations immediately. Then they only have temporary problems which do not become secrets. They do not deny. If they don't have the answer to the problem, they look for it.

The not-so-perfect family denies there's a problem to deal with. Then it becomes a secret—and thus a problem. Most parents from not-so-perfect families were also raised in families that were not-so-perfect. They were never shown how to deal with stressful situations. If we also deny the problems in our families, they could become secrets. As we get older and begin a family, we could be in the same spot as our parents, passing on problems over and over again until someone finally says, "Hey, there's a problem here. Let's deal with it."

Finding out what our family secrets are can be difficult. There are a lot of distractions. The roles we are appointed are a major distraction from the problem. When I was a scapegoat, my behavior was the visible problem—not my father's denial of his father's alcoholism. The more I acted out, the more I was the problem—without realizing I was protecting the family secrets and drawing all the attention to myself.

Remember the situation where I went running down the street yelling, *"What's wrong with me?"* and looking for a way to fix it? Well, if I would have been aware of family secrets and how my family operated, I would have at least understood that the problem wasn't me. I have figured out that the real secret wasn't just that my grandfather was an alcoholic. He had *abandoned* my father when my father was fifteen years old. This left my father depressed nearly all his life, and unable to show feelings of love and affection for me, his firstborn son. Now I understand that he never received what he also deserved: a loving father. How could he pass on to me what he never received himself? He could only have done this if he had brought this family secret into the open, dealt with his feelings, and—like me—learned how his family operated.

You may have guessed by now that chemical dependency is a major family secret for a lot of families. One out of four young people are affected by chemical dependency in their family. If there are twenty students in a classroom, five of them are affected by a family member who abuses drugs or alcohol.

## Sexual Abuse

Another major family secret is sexual abuse. Anytime a parent, an older brother or sister, aunt or uncle use a child for anything sexual, it is a form of *sexual abuse* called *incest*. This is one of the hardest family secrets to bring into the open. Besides most people being uptight about discussing sex, a young person may also fear losing a relationship with someone he or she loves and seeks approval from—a parent or a favorite relative.

Incest tends to begin early in the child's life. Only when a child reaches their teenage years do they realize incest *isn't* normal. Then they feel as though they must make this a secret because they have been fooled into believing they willingly took part in the abuse. This puts a young person in a real bind. They feel confused and dirty. They may turn to alcohol and drugs, and become depressed and suicidal. Some young victims of incest lose the real meaning of sex and begin using it as a tool to get what they want—eventually getting into prostitution.

Yet another form of sexual abuse that affects young people and often becomes a secret is *rape*. Rape is forced sexual involvement that is very traumatic. This trauma comes about because of what usually happens during the rape: that is, the threat of *physical abuse,* of being hurt or killed if they resist. This can be too much for the rape victim to take. Many of them try to deny the rape happened, or say "It's over...I'll just forget it." If they do tell their parents, it's possible they won't be believed. The same types of problems encountered by the victim of family sexual abuse often develop.

## Misty's Story

The following is a story of rape which was quickly turned into a secret. The writer of the story is Misty (not her real name). She is a friend of mine. Misty offered me permission to reprint her story in the hopes it might spare another young rape victim the kind of suffering she experienced:

> I worked for a friend of the family at the gas station he owned in the small town I grew up in. I was fourteen at the time. I was in the process of buying a guitar and wanted money to pay it off. I enjoyed having the responsibility, and the money coming in wasn't bad. I was used to baby-sitting for my extra cash. I got fifty cents an hour. The two dollars and fifty cents I got working at the gas station seemed like gold to me.
>
> The attention I got from my employer was great for my ego. He was very good at listening to my problems. I could talk to him, and it seemed like I had a good friend in him. There were plenty of times I talked to him about boyfriends or family troubles, and he was always there for me. I was feeling pretty adult with all this as my parents had no time for serious conversation with me. Dad was on some kind of pain killer that made him very emotional. My mom had just recovered from a bout with cancer. There was a lot of stress in my family. I felt very lost in the shuffle. I wanted desperately to be loved.
>
> I was already experimenting with my sexual feeling, and my current boyfriend was busy enjoying it. I think some of it was normal, but it was starting to get a little heavy. I broke away from him, not feeling close, still in search of something to fill the emptiness.

My boss knew of everything that went on in my life, and he was good at finding the right words to make me feel better. At one point, he began making comments that were inappropriate. But the attention was so overwhelming that I chose to revel in it.

Somewhere between Christmas and New Years he began making physical advances towards me. I shunned them and began to feel very uncomfortable. I was aroused by the thought that a grown man would be interested in me. He was around thirty-five years old. Since I was fourteen, his advances made me feel pretty grown up. Nevertheless, I knew it was not OK. He was married with two children. I had even gone shopping for him to get his wife a birthday present. I felt very trusted and mature. I was also very confused. My body was responding to the thought of being physical with this man, but my conscience was telling me to be true to myself and save my virginity.

My boss found ways for us to be alone. I became frightened and tried to avoid him without letting him think I didn't appreciate his kindness and friendship. I wasn't sure what to do. What was right and what wasn't? I had no idea how to handle my emotions, much less his moves towards physical intimacy. It was too much to discuss even with my best friend. I was beginning to feel ashamed. How had I provoked all this?

Then it happened. The confrontation I had begun to fear.

I had no idea when he asked me to type some index cards after the station closed that he had other things on his mind. I had grown accustomed to his leering remarks and gestures, so I figured I'd just fend them off again if anything got out of hand. I really had no clue to the extent of the difficulty I was in.

It became quite clear almost immediately that cold evening. It was nearly 5:30 P.M., and my boss closed up the station as he normally did. He then proceeded to explain what he wanted me to do.

With great labor, he explained in detail the index file system he wanted me to devise. In the process, he began making close contact with me by leaning over me, seducing me. He talked in a low voice, pressing up against my back. Then I became extremely uncomfortable, and I started to feel panic. As I got up from the desk, he calmly walked towards me until I was backed up against some pop bottles stacked against the wall. I started to fall, and then he tried to kiss me and touch me. "All I want to do is be loved," I said. That was all he wanted, too.

I knew he didn't understand, and I tried to explain it to him. But he was too overcome with his own selfish desires, and I begged him to stop and to listen to me. He continued his advances, not wanting to hear what I was saying.

I was afraid of what was about to happen—and frightened of someone walking in and blaming me for the disgusting predicament I was in. I was overwhelmed with humiliation, shame, and guilt. But most of all, I felt sheer terror at my inability to do anything to stop the violation I was feeling.

I remember wondering what I would do if his wife walked in. I imagined being able to crawl out of a small door at the bottom of the wall in the bathroom he now pushed me into.

The floor was filthy. The smell of the oil from the garage was pungent and assaulted my nostrils. The paint on the walls was peeling. The toilet looked like it hadn't been cleaned in weeks. I knew it was the bathroom the employees used. They were all men except for me, and I felt mortified by their unkept ways. Only men could be such swine. I think that, for the first time, I truly felt hate. I thought of his wife and kids. I felt sorry for them. Did they have any idea what kind of man they loved?

As he pulled me down and raped me, I felt rage well up inside me and pour through every living part of my body and soul. I knew it would be over soon, but then the pain shot through me, and I cried for him to stop. But he was begging me just to hold on a little bit longer. It would be over before I knew it, he said.

All I could do was squeeze my eyes shut and pray for forgiveness from his wife, his kids, and from God.

Then it was over. As I stood up, unaware of what he had left inside me, he quickly told me to sit down on the toilet and clean up. I began to panic that I would be pregnant, and he told me that he had had a vasectomy. What a guy, I thought. How nice and convenient for him. Was this so he could go around forcing himself on whoever he pleased?

Not being able to comprehend the actions of this man, the unbearable shame, or the flood of tears I shed, I began searching for an escape from my emotions. I knew he kept a bottle of liquor in his desk. He was a recovering alcoholic and in a program. But apparently, like everything else in his life, he had his own rules. I never let on that I knew about it. It was the perfect solution to ease the incredible sadness I was experiencing.

I found the bottle and drank as much as my stomach could handle. I began feeling somewhat calmer and more in control. I knew the release it would give me.

After getting drunk, I walked home in a stupor. I had to appear OK to my parents or they would become suspicious. I was scared. Nothing could change that.

I stopped by my best friend's house to sort out the craziness. She was strong and compassionate. She was everything I needed at that moment. She listened and still loved me. I was relieved and grateful.

My parents called her house looking for me, so I went home ready to face the music. My dad started ranting and raving about me not coming home right away. They were upset because my mom had kept my dinner in the oven to stay warm. As usual, I was the ungrateful child who just expected everyone to build their lives around mine. I began crying hysterically, begging my father to stop yelling. But he just kept it up, drilling me with questions and insults. I told him between sobs that he just didn't understand what I had been through. He slapped me and screamed that I was being melodramatic.

The anger and shock sent me reeling. I swore from that point on I would never tell my parents. I quit work the next day and no one asked any questions. After a month, it seemed like the whole incident never happened. Then I lost memory of it altogether.

My friend didn't mention it again either, so I suppose there was really nothing to remind me. I did know, however, that I hated my ex-boss fiercely, and I was extremely depressed. I drank whenever I could. I had terrible problems with anxiety, insecurity, and promiscuity.

Years have passed since I was raped. I did well in keeping my shameful secret deeply hidden until my last drunk four years ago—not that two bad marriages or many failed relationships didn't give some indication of my intimacy problems. Drinking and drugs were just a symptom of the underlying conflicts. I have spent a great deal of time talking with professionals to work through the events of my childhood so I can become a healthier, happier, and more sincere person. It has been well worth the effort to finally believe that I was a victim—and not the instigator. I finally am free. I still grieve for losing the little girl inside me. But I am free of the deep-rooted suffering the rape has caused throughout my life. I believe the little girl in me deserves the right to smile again.

And she does.


It is understandable how this story became a deep dark family secret. It is unfortunate that Misty had to continue suffering for so many years. Although she wishes she would have dealt with it much earlier, Misty has faced her codependency.


## Physical/Verbal Abuse

Physical abuse is one of the other major problems that becomes a family secret. This is yet another example of how a problem is passed on to us if our parent or parents haven't dealt with it. I include verbal abuse along with physical abuse because it usually happens at the same time. Verbal abuse does happen without being physically hurt, but its emotional effects are just as devastating. Physical scars heal in time. But the scars left by being told things like "You're no good," "I wish you were never born," or "You'll never amount to anything" can affect us for a lifetime. Physical abuse can be more traumatic if the abuse is so extreme that an arm or a leg is broken , or there is a real risk of being killed through continued beatings.

Young people are being abused in our society. We don't have to put up with it. We can do something about it. Physical abuse is not only wrong, it is illegal.

§

I vowed I wouldn't tell young people what to do when writing this book. I wanted to offer some helpful information, and let the reader take it from there. But this is my one exception to my vow. Physical abuse can be a scary thing to escape from. Many young people don't. *If you are presently being abused, you need to get out.* You do this by telling someone. Your minister, doctor, school teacher, local welfare department, or a close adult friend can help. It may be a hassle, but there is help for you and your family. Although you don't know me and I don't know you, I do care about what happens to you. I care because I was one of those young people who was physically and verbally abused.

## A Personal Abuse Story

I was so thrilled to be going to Grandma's house again. I was about five years old, and the first thing I would do when I got there was go down into the basement, reach into a big barrel, and grab a handful of sweet pickles. My grandmother made the best sweet pickles in the world, and I could almost taste them as I approached the door.

When I knocked on the door, grandma opened it. I began to walk in, smiling from ear-to-ear, happy to be there and anxious to get at the sweet pickles.

Grandma drew back her arm and hit me square on the face with her open hand.

"Ouch!" I screamed.

I was confused and began to ask her what I had done when she hit me again even *harder*. "Shut up!" she yelled.

Then she called me a brat and told me to stay out of the pickles.

Scenes like this were repeated over and over for many years of my young life. My grandmother was not the only abuser. There was another relative. He would tease and humiliate me whenever he got the chance—which was often. This relative would baby-sit me quite a bit. Then he would do things like put my soiled underpants over my head and make me wear them like that all day. This was supposed to help me learn not to wet my pants.

As a result of the abuse, I felt worthless and defective. I developed an extreme nervousness which showed in my speech. I stuttered so badly that I could hardly be understood. I also became a bed-wetter. This continued into my teenage years which, along with my stuttering, was a daily embarrassment.

During my elementary school days, I was teased constantly for my stuttering and smelly clothes. I had to fight my way home almost every day after school, for there was always someone waiting for me along the way to tease me. All of this left me feeling constant fear and rage. I was afraid of the dark. I didn't trust anyone because it seemed no one was there to protect me. In truth, there wasn't.

Eventually, this anger was directed at my father. I blamed him for not being there to protect me. I could easily justify everything I did from that point on—like stealing my dad's booze or my parent's money. I eventually justified hating the whole world— which I did for many years. But the person I hated the most was me. No wonder. I was *taught* to hate me—taught by the abusers who were probably abused themselves. They passed it on to an innocent, lovable, five-year-old boy who just wanted to have fun at grandma's house.

This abuse is still a family secret. I ask my parents from time to time if they remember anything about this. "Maybe your uncle didn't like you too much," my mother said, "but I don't think he abused you." My dad doesn't seem to want to talk about it at all.

I don't need my parents to tell me it happened. I *know* it happened. With help, I've learned to love again—especially that innocent five-year-old boy. He's not being abused or abusing himself anymore.

## Domestic Violence

Another physical/verbal abuse situation that becomes a secret is when one or both of our parents are physically and verbally abusing one or the other. I used an example of this earlier in the book. We may feel responsible, become insecure, and blame ourselves because we're afraid our parents will abandon us. Believe me, it's not us that is the problem, it's them. We can learn not to have their problems affect us. We can learn what we can and cannot do to help our parents stop fighting. This is called *detachment*. We'll learn a good deal about this in the *Recovery* chapter of the book.

Without learning detachment from a problem such as this early in our life, we risk buying into the idea that it's OK to settle arguments with violence. We also risk believing that we can get people to do what we want if we threaten them or hit them. This may already have begun if you have ever threatened to hit a girl or boy you have or are dating. Some people call this "fatal attraction." It's not. It's just another example of passing on what's been passed on to us—in this case, the false belief that we can control other people with our behavior. The scary part is, it can be—and too many times is—fatal if continued into our adulthood.

§

Keeping secrets is one way our family can affect us. The *messages and rules* we receive from them is another way they can affect us—and that is the topic of the next chapter.

## Suggested Activities:

•Make a list of what you think are some of your family secrets.

_____

_____

_____

_____

_____

_____

_____

•If your parents are in recovery and they are willing to talk about some of the secrets, give it a try—talk about how these secrets have affected you.

•If these secrets are too scary to talk about with your parents, talk with a counselor or trusted friend.

•If you don't feel ready to deal with these secrets yet, that's OK. Find a support program. You'll find more information on them in the *Resources for Recovery* chapter of this book.

*What's Wrong With Me?*

**Chapter Four**

# *Messages and Rules*

This chapter is about messages and rules—not just the obvious rules like "If you don't come home by ten o'clock, you'll be grounded!" or "If you break the law, you'll go to jail!" I'm talking about the rules that direct our lives. These rules are made up of messages that come into our heads and tell us things like what we should believe in (our values), our personal value to the world (self-worth), and how we should behave towards others.

We get these messages throughout our life from three major sources: our family, society, and our friends (peers).

## Family Messages

Most of the messages and ultimate rules that direct our lives come from our family. The kinds of messages (and whether they help or hurt us) depend on the type of family we're raised in. In not-so-perfect families, we can and do get some confusing and false messages.

As a young boy, the only way I learned things was from copying my parents—especially my father. Whenever I said something like repeat a bad word he used, he would yell at me and say, "Do as I say, not as I do." I think many parents today believe in using this message. What they can't seem to understand is that it just doesn't work. A more accurate message might be: "Monkey see, monkey do!"

Another example from my family which was very hurtful and totally false was, "You're limited in what you can do, so don't go for your dreams because you can't possibly reach them." I remember a conversation I had with my father when I was about fourteen years old. I was confused about what I wanted to be when I grew up. I brought up a number of things like doctor, lawyer, and scientist. My father responded by saying, "Lonny, you have to understand, you're limited. You're not like other people. You stutter." Then he said, "Besides, we're poor, and everyone is against us. We're one of the have-not families. You'll never make it. The odds are against you."

I realize that my father was trying to make sure I didn't get hurt pursuing "impossible" dreams. He didn't—and still doesn't—understand that he was passing on his own messages of hopelessness from his childhood. He had never had the experience of overcoming obstacles like poverty and low self-esteem. He had lost whatever dreams he may have had as a child. He, like me, didn't have a father who would say things like: "Go for it. You can do whatever you set your mind to do. I'm behind you all the way."

## Physical Messages in Families

There are other ways messages are passed on to us. A hug is a physical message of love, acceptance, and nurturing. Physical messages let us know we are being cared for, and that we're worthwhile. A slap on the face gives us the message that we are deserving of abuse, that we are flawed or defective. Sexual involvement within the family leads to messages such as: "The only way to feel loved is through sex" or "The only way to get what I want is to be seductive and sexual."

Healthy families give each member lots of hugs and pats on the back—something my family never learned to do, except with the females. The message here is: "Guys don't hug and show affection." Somehow, this might make them feel uncool. But guess what? Hugging feels good. I've learned to love hugs. They make me feel like I'm not alone, that someone's with me no matter how bad I might feel.

## Family Roles and Messages

Many of the messages we receive come from the roles we are appointed in our family. The hero learns to "Do the family proud" and "Be perfect—don't make mistakes." The scapegoat learns "You're the problem" and "You'll never amount to anything." The lost child learns that "Nobody cares about me, therefore I must be worthless." And the mascot learns that "I must be a failure if I can't entertain everyone."

## Family Rules

When these messages are repeated over and over again, they become *rules*. We may not always be consciously aware these rules are there, but they are. They are controlling a good deal of what we do, the way we look at ourselves, and the way we view other people.

Fortunately, there are healthy rules made up of healthy messages (like *Do unto others as you would have them do unto you*) that most of us have operating in our heads besides the unhealthy ones. The problem is, the unhealthy ones are more rigidly stuck in our heads—and there are more of them for those of us who are from not-so-perfect families.

Here are some family rules that are unhealthy.* See if you can identify the ones in *your* family:

> •Don't feel. Don't talk about feelings. Don't express feelings. Guys, it's okay for you to feel angry, but don't feel hurt or scared. Be macho.
>
> •Don't think. You can't make good decisions.
>
> •Don't talk about problems. Don't identify problems. Don't solve problems.
>
> •Don't be who you are. Be "good," "right," "strong" and "perfect."
>
> •Don't be selfish. Don't pay attention to what you want and need. Take care of other people. Don't be responsible for yourself.

*Based on family rules developed by Robert Subby and John Friel in "Co-dependency—a Paradoxical Codependency," *Codependency, An Emerging Issue*, Health Communications (1984).

•Don't have fun, don't be silly, and don't enjoy life. It isn't necessary.

•Don't trust people. Don't trust yourself. Don't be vulnerable.

•Don't be direct. Manipulate to get what you want or need—or have someone else do it for you.

•Don't get close to people. Judge them. Criticize them.

•Don't grow, change, or do anything that might rock the family boat—even if doing so is appropriate and in your best interest (in other words, don't talk about family secrets).

## Messages from Society

Society is made up of all kinds of people from all types of cultures and families. These people live and work in our communities, neighborhoods, and hometowns. They're our neighbors. They make up the media (television, radio, videos, newspapers, and movies). They're the teachers in our schools, the police officers, the judges, and the writers of the books we read. Society's messages have a major impact on us as we're growing up.

Here are some messages I've picked up recently: "Our young people are out-of-control." "They're running our streets and threatening old people." "Teenagers aren't learning anything in school. They'll never amount to anything."

You may or may not be picking up these exact messages, but it's important to understand that a lot of people are—people like our parents, teachers, neighbors, and police. Society has this problem with blaming groups of people for things that only a few of them do.

When I was about fifteen years old, I bought into this message: "Young people in groups are not to be trusted." I ran with a gang in my hometown. It was natural for me because I had already bought into the message of being an irresponsible rebel. We, the gang, did what we wanted in the streets. We stole gas from cars, we stole booze and drank, and we stole drugs and used them. Well, we didn't last long. After a year, we were all arrested (the police were watching us, compiling evidence the entire time). Some of us were locked up. Others, like myself, were put on probation.

My criminal career stopped right there. But for many young people, it doesn't. Since then, I've figured out that I was buying in to messages from society about teens. I was a puppet being controlled by other people and always getting the short end of the stick. I'm making my own decisions now. They're right for me. They're healthy decisions—and they're mine. I trust them.

You can do the same.

# Racism

Racism is one of society's worst examples of how it passes on hurtful and false messages. These messages say that if we're different in some way from the majority, then somehow we're inferior (less equal).

Let's look at society as one big not-so-perfect family. This big family needs a scapegoat to take attention off the real problems. Society's scapegoat is its minorities. There are many minority groups affected by these messages. But the ones I see affected the most today are Afro-Americans, Native Americans, and women.

I don't pretend to have the answers to racism. But I can tell you something about the negative messages that are being passed on about minorities: they're all lies, and they're destructive. No matter what our color or sex, we're all human beings.

I understand the anger many people from these groups feel. It's truly unfair being made society's scapegoats. I also understand the battle waged by many minority groups to obtain what is already supposed to be equal rights. Here are some suggestions to help win this battle:

•Don't buy into society's messages.

•Learn more about your culture from people within who have pride in who they are.

•Realize that, as scapegoats, we hurt ourselves by acting out in ways that society can point a finger and say, "See, I told you they're no good!"

## The Media

"To be cool, you have to look slim." "To get the good-looking ladies, you have to look like a weightlifter." These are a couple of messages from society that are delivered through the media. Here's another: "It's cool to drink beer because all our sports heroes do." Have you ever seen a sports event on T.V. that didn't have at least five beer commercials in it? How about the message "Just say 'no' to drugs." It would be nice if it were that easy. This message fails to tell us *how* to say 'no' when our lives are all screwed up and all we've learned to trust is drugs and alcohol.

Since this book is part of the media, I would like to pass on a few of my own messages to you:

> •Young people can and do make healthy decisions. They constantly strive to be the best people they can.

> •Young people care about our world and the people in it.

> •Young people of today are talented. If we—the adults—believe in them, they can do anything. Even when we don't, many young people succeed despite this lack of support.

## Single-Parent Families

I think the young people and the parent from single-parent families are getting a raw deal from society and the media. I hear this message over and over: "The reason young people are having so many problems today is because they are being raised in single-parent families." I realize it can be hard at times. It's very difficult for the parent to make ends meet, and not feel guilty about not spending enough time with their children.

But single-parent families do just fine. They have to work closely together to overcome many obstacles. By doing so, the young person and their parent end up believing in themselves and their ability to handle anything that comes along.

If you're from a single-parent family and you don't think things are going so well, don't worry. You'll do just fine—if you work closely with your parent.

## Messages From Our Peers

Many people in society today are saying that *peer pressure* is what makes young people do just about everything: drugs, crime, getting pregnant—you name it. It was important for me to be accepted by my friends, and I suspect it is the same for you. It is also true that I responded to my friends' messages to do something I really knew wasn't cool just to gain acceptance. But when I began doing drugs and alcohol, there was more behind it than some friend telling me to do it. I felt like a nobody. I felt stressed out. I had been abused, and I was in pain. I was *already* knocking on the door to drug abuse; my friends let me in.

Here are some things we might ask ourselves when our friends ask us to take part in something we really know isn't OK:

•Does this thing really go against what I believe in?

•Where can I go for support if I go against what they want me to do?

•If I go along with this, am I just buying into all these messages I'm learning about?

•Am I being operated like a puppet on a string?

## Shame and Guilt

I've always noticed how we use these two words at the same time, as if they mean the same thing. They really are two different things.

Guilt is a healthy emotion that we feel when we do something that we really don't believe in, something that goes against our values. We all have done and will continue to do things that we will feel guilty about.

Guilt is all about our behavior. If I believe it's not OK to steal, but go ahead and steal something, I will feel guilty. I can learn how to deal with this by eventually choosing not to steal. It's fairly easy to get rid of these guilty feelings when they happen. It's not so easy when we feel shame.

Shame occurs when we make a mistake (which is human)—and then think we *are* a mistake, a flawed and defective person. What makes this happen is all the stuff we've been talking about up to this point: having negative, hurtful, and false messages passed on to us over and over again. For many of us who have been buying into these messages, it is difficult to fight off shame.

Through our involvement in recovery programs, we do succeed. What we use to fight off these messages is *affirmations*. These are also messages, but positive ones. There is a list of these affirmations and a discussion on how to use them in the *Recovery* section of this book. Here's one to start you off: "You're OK just the way you are."

I know it's hard to believe completely that we're OK just the way we are by saying it once—especially if we've been told over and over that we are *not* OK. That's why we need to repeat these positive messages over and over when one of the negative ones pops into our head.

Up till now, we've been talking about things that bring about stress and pain in our lives. In the next chapter, we'll learn about how many of us *react* to this stress. We'll talk about how we've learned to survive this stress by taking on *codependent survival behaviors* which may at times be compulsive, even addictive. Finally, you'll be able to *understand* your own codependency and learn how to deal with it.

## Suggested Activities:

During the next week, take a small notebook with you wherever you go. Divide each page by using the headings *Messages from Family*, *Messages from Society*, and *Messages from Peers*. Further divide each of these with *Positive* and *Negative* (see the example on the next page). Keep track of all the messages you hear. Hold onto these and add to them as you wish. We'll do some adjusting of these when we get into the *Recovery* section.

|  | Positive Messages | Negative Messages |
|---|---|---|
| Family | We're proud of you! | You're no good. |
| Peers | You're cool. | You're a loser. |
| Society | The community needs you. | You can't be trusted. |

## Chapter Five

# *Codependent Survival Behavior*

What we've been talking about up to this point is our developing codependency. We've learned a lot about what brings on emotional pain and stress. We have discovered how many of us feel flawed, defective, hurt, angry, and alone. We have also learned why many of us are struggling to trust others, and why all this stuff has been passed on to us. What we need to discuss now is how we attempt to survive all this confusion and pain by taking on certain *codependent survival behaviors*.

In the preceding chapter, I pointed out some examples of codependent survival behavior. In this chapter, I will be very specific. This will help us better understand our own codependency issues.

I'm going to do this by first restating the definition of adolescent codependency and breaking it into four parts. Using the following *Codependency Charts*, we'll talk about the main codependent survival behaviors that cause us problems.

> *Adolescent codependency is (2) __emotional stress, confu-sion, fear, and pain__ brought on by (1) __events__ in our family and society which __messes up__ our healthy development into adulthood. Our reaction is to take on one or more (3) __survival behaviors.__ These behaviors, together with the events that set them up, are (4) __passed on__ from generation to generation through our families and society.*

There are many more events that happen which I have not listed in the charts—perhaps hundreds. I used those that happen most often and cause the most problems. Take some time to read the brief explanation that accompanies each chart. You will find yourself using this information to help you figure out and understand your codependency—even after you have finished the book.

## Codependency Chart #1
## Family Alcohol & Drug Abuse

This chart shows what can happen in the **Event** that a *family member develops alcohol and drug problems.* When this happens, we can experience many painful **Feelings** like *anger, loneliness, and guilt.* To deal with these feelings, we may develop a variety of **Adolescent Codependent Survival Behaviors** like denying, blaming, and lying. If we do not find a healthy way to deal with these behaviors, they can develop into **Adult Codependent Survival Behaviors** like *compulsive lying* and *criminal behavior.*

# Codependency Chart #1
# Family Alcohol & Drug Abuse

| (1) Event | (2) Feelings | (3) Adolescent Codependent Survival Behavior | (4) Adult Codependent Survival Behavior |
|---|---|---|---|
| •Family member(s) develop(s) alcohol & drug problems. | •Hurt<br><br>Mistrusted<br><br>Angry<br><br>Confused<br><br>Rejected<br><br>Lonely<br><br>Guilty<br><br>Shame<br><br>Abandoned<br><br>Inadequate<br><br>Defective<br><br>Confused<br><br>Hopeless<br><br>Depressed<br><br>Fearful<br><br>Unloved | **Denial**<br>•Deny to self and others that there is a problem.<br>•Deny problem is bad, thinking it will stop soon.<br>•Stay busy and not think about it; use music without knowing why (compulsively).<br><br>**Caretaking**<br>•Be a better kid; do more at school; be perfect.<br><br>•Blame yourself, not the person with the problem.<br><br>•Blame others.<br><br>•Lie for the person so they don't get in trouble.<br><br>**Unmet Needs**<br>•Lying to get needs met to survive (manipulating).<br>•Hook-up to any peer group who will accept us (low self-esteem).<br>•Cutting, burning self for attention (self-abusive).<br>•Running away because of fear and for attention.<br>•Go from one relationship to another seeking approval. | •Continue denying despite major crises.<br>•Make up excuses thinking it will soon stop.<br>•Become a workaholic or super volunteer; use religion compulsively.<br><br><br><br>•Be a better wife/husband; cook better, clean more.<br><br>•Believe you are the problem.<br><br>•Become judgmental/martyr.<br><br>•Become totally involved in the enabler role.<br><br><br>•Compulsive lying even when there is no need.<br>•Possible criminal behavior.<br><br><br>•Screaming, yelling, going crazy for attention.<br>•Fear of commitment; many divorces/break ups.<br>•Relationship addiction. |

## Codependency Chart #2
## More About Family Alcohol & Drug Abuse

Chart #2 shows more negative results of a family member's alcohol and drug problem—specifically when our needs are not met. To fill our needs, we may start buying things without reason (compulsively). We may become sexually active, or we may start to overeat. This can lead to compulsive shopping, sexual addiction, or constant (chronic) obesity by the time we become adults—if we're not already affected by these behaviors.

# Codependency Chart #2
# More About Family Alcohol & Drug Abuse

| (1) Event | (2) Feelings | (3) Adolescent Codependent Survival Behavior | (4) Adult Codependent Survival Behavior |
|---|---|---|---|
| | | **Unmet Needs** | |
| •Family member(s) develop(s) alcohol & drug problems. | •Hurt<br><br>Mistrusted<br><br>Angry<br><br>Confused<br><br>Rejected<br><br>Lonely<br><br>Guilty<br><br>Shame<br><br>Abandoned<br><br>Inadequate<br><br>Defective<br><br>Confused<br><br>Hopeless<br><br>Depressed<br><br>Fearful<br><br>Unloved | •Seeking material items compulsively to help improve self-esteem.<br><br>•Frequently being sexual with partners for approval and physical pleasure.<br><br>•Purging food to feel better about self and gain some control.<br>•Overeating to fill emptiness caused by feeling unloved.<br>•Becoming pregnant for someone to love and for someone to love us.<br>•Chemical & alcohol use for good feelings (develop love relationship with chemicals).<br><br>•Become extremely rebellious for attention.<br><br><br>•Physically and verbally lash out against all types of authority; fighting, criminal behavior; violent behavior in relationships. | •Compulsive shopping.<br><br>•Sexual addiction, prostitution.<br><br>•Chronic dieting, anorexia, bulimia, and possibly death.<br><br>•Chronic obesity; constantly overweight; always dieting; food addiction.<br>•Poverty/welfare becomes a way-of-life.<br><br>•Chronic alcohol and drug addiction; physical/psychological dependence.<br><br>•Labelled a troublemaker at work and in the community; get into legal trouble.<br><br>•Criminal behavior becomes way-of-life; long-term prison; perpetrator or victim of domestic violence (perhaps both). |

49

## Codependency Chart #3
## Depression & Physical/Verbal Abuse

Here we can see how depression can affect us when a family member has a drug/alcohol problem. We may decide to hide our feelings from others—as well as ourselves. This can cause persistent depression when we get older. We may start to gamble for thrills. This could lead to a gambling addiction. Or we may start to think about suicide as a way to kill our depressed feelings. If we are lucky enough to make it to our adult years, thoughts of suicide might become constant.

This chart also shows us what can happen in the **Event** that we are exposed to *physical or verbal abuse*. We may become sad or feel defective. To deal with these painful feelings, we may find ourselves being *self-abusive* or even developing *criminal behavior*. This can lead to *future physical problems* or a *life of crime*.

# Codependency Chart #3
# Depression & Physical/Verbal Abuse

| (1) Event | (2) Feelings | (3) Adolescent Codependent Survival Behavior | (4) Adult Codependent Survival Behavior |
|---|---|---|---|
| | | **Depression** | |
| •Family member(s) develop(s) alcohol & drug problems. | | •Stuff (internalize) feelings. | •Chronic depression. |
| | | •Compulsively seeks ways to feel high. Drugs, sex, or excitement to fight off depression. | •Prescription drug abuse and possible addiction. Sexual and/or excitement obsession. |
| | | •Gambling for high to fight off depression. | •Gambling addiction. |
| | | •Suicidal thinking; preoccupation with suicide to escape pain. | •Compulsively preoccupied with suicide; cry frequently for no apparent reason; stress-related physical problems. |
| •Physical/verbal abuse. | •Fear Hurt Sad Angry Mistrustful Shame Defective Inadequate Depressed | •Withdrawn/isolated; become a loner; depressed; suicidal thinking. | •Chronically depressed and hopeless. |
| | | •Become physically and verbally controlling in our relationships; intimidate and threaten to get our way, or put up with it if it happens to us. | •Become a perpetrator or a victim of physical/verbal abuse. |
| | | •Self-abusive; poor personal hygiene because of extreme feelings of being defective. | •Physical health problems because of not looking after self. |
| | | •Running away (may make sense at the time). | •Fear of commitments; numerous relationships. |
| | | •Criminal behavior; refuse to trust anyone in a position of authority (teachers get a lot of our rage). | •Criminal behavior may become a way of life; early death very possible. |
| | | •Stealing and other criminal behavior for the adrenaline high. | •Compulsive/addictive criminal behavior. |

# Codependency Chart #4
# Sexual Abuse

This chart deals with the **Event** of *sexual abuse*. *Shame*, *guilt*, and other painful feelings can result, and we may turn to survival behaviors like *aggressive sexual play* and *drug use* to kill the pain. Without dealing with these issues, we can become *sexually abusive* and *addicted to drugs* by the time we are adults—if we haven't already begun this process.

# Codependency Chart #4
# Sexual Abuse

| (1) Event | (2) Feelings | (3) Adolescent Codependent Survival Behavior | (4) Adult Codependent Survival Behavior |
|---|---|---|---|
| •Physical/verbal abuse. | | •Alcohol and drug dependency at an early age.<br><br>**All other behaviors associated with alcohol and drug events listed above are possible.** | •Chronic alcohol and drug addiction. |
| •Being sexually abused (including incest and rape). | •Shame<br>Guilty<br>Mistrustful<br>Dirty<br>Angry<br>Depressed<br>Confused | •Deny that it happened.<br><br>•Seductive manipulation; promiscuity; prostitution.<br><br>•Not able to accept "no" from partner when wanting sex; date rape; belief that the only way to give or receive love is through sex.<br><br>•Aggressive sexual play to release pent-up anger.<br><br>•Attraction to partners who are highly sexual.<br><br>•Become depressed; attempt suicide to reach out.<br><br>•Alcohol and drug usage; possible dependency.<br><br>•Become obese to avoid sex.<br><br>**All other behaviors listed under *Family Member(s) Develop Alcohol & DrugProblem(s)* are possible.** | •Stress-related health problems.<br><br>•Seduction and sex become the only way to get needs met; sex addiction.<br><br>•Perpetrator of rape; sexual attraction to children; belief that the only way to give or receive love is through sex.<br><br>•Become involved in abusive sexual play; possible physical harm.<br><br>•Marry sex abuse victims or perpetrators.<br><br>•Suicidal thinking; attempts may succeed.<br><br>•Alcohol and drug addiction.<br><br>•Obesity to avoid sex. |

## Codependency Chart #5
## Messages, Family Secrets & Peer Pressure

Chart #5 deals with three different **Events:** *false and confusing messages, family secrets,* and *peer pressure.*

*Receiving false and confusing messages* can cause us to feel *angry* and *confused.* Our response may be to *rebel against authority,* or we may decide *not to care about the world around us* (apathy). This may be causing us problems already—and may cause us even more problems as adults. Our *job performance may suffer,* or we may become *anti-social.*

*Keeping family secrets* can cause all kinds of painful *feelings* and *behaviors.* Since we don't know what the secret is, we can't identify the problem.

*Receiving peer pressure* can also cause all kinds of bad *feelings* and *behaviors.*

# Codependency Chart #5
# Messages, Family Secrets & Peer Pressure

| (1) Event | (2) Feelings | (3) Adolescent Codependent Survival Behavior | (4) Adult Codependent Survival Behavior |
|---|---|---|---|
| •Receiving false and confusing messages from society (racism and the view that kids are bad). | •Mistrustful Confused Anger Inadequate | •Rebel against authority; do poorly in school. <br><br> •Don't care about what is going on in the world or community. | •Criminal behavior; low productivity at work. <br><br> •Become either anti-social or an extreme activist unwilling to accept compromise. |
| •Keeping family secrets. | •Any and all feelings are possible. | **All survival behaviors are possible because the secret is not known. It may be buried for generations. This does not stop the secret from being acted out by one of our children.** | |
| •Receiving peer pressure. | •Any and all feelings are possible. | **Being teased by our peers for our survival behavior (being overweight, etc.) can reinforce all the bad feelings we're trying to escape. Peer pressure (to use alcohol and drugs, for example) gives us permission to escape (temporarily) from these feelings. Most of these friends are probably trying to escape the same situations and feelings. We seek out peer groups who give us the OK to use any—if not all—of our survival behaviors.** | |

## Codependency Chart #6
## Non-Traditional Religious Practices

Finally, we have the **Event** of *becoming involved with shaming and religious practices.* This involvement can give us feelings of *shame, guilt* and *inadequacy,* and cause us to seek unrealistic goals of *perfection* or *pursue occult activities.* This rebelliousness can lead to *self-righteousness* or *long-term involvement in non-traditional spiritual practices* by the time we're adults.

# Codependency Chart #6
# Non-Traditional Religious Practices

| (1) Event | (2) Feelings | (3) Adolescent Codependent Survival Behavior | (4) Adult Codependent Survival Behavior |
|---|---|---|---|
| •Becoming involved with shaming and punishing religious practices. | •Shame Guilt Anger Fear Inadequate Mistrustful | •Perfection; doing everything right.<br><br>•Self-punishing because we are not always able to be perfect.<br><br>•Depressed; suicidal thinking.<br><br>•Rebellious/criminal behavior; chemical abuse.<br><br>•Pursue activities related to the occult or what society calls evil. | •Perfectionism; self-righteousness; compulsively religious.<br><br>•Physical illness related to stress; belief that we are evil.<br><br>•Medicate depression with drugs; possible suicide.<br><br>•Chemical dependency; criminal behavior.<br><br>•Long-term involvement in non-traditional spiritual practices. |

## Putting It All Together

Before we put together all the parts to figure out what our individual codependency looks like, there are a few things we need to consider.

*Often, we have more than one event happening in our lives at the same time.* It is not unusual to have physical abuse, verbal abuse, and sexual abuse combined with alcohol and drug abuse problems in a family. In my own life, I had alcoholism, physical/ verbal abuse, and confusing messages from society. This made my *codependent survival behaviors* more intense and compulsive and set me up to develop more of them.

*Although our survival behavior can become self-destructive, it usually makes sense at the time.* An example: For an **Event**, let's use *family member develops alcohol & drug abuse problems*; for **Feelings**, let's use *confused.* Our **Adolescent Codependent Survival Behavior** is to *deny* the problem. *Confused* means just that. We don't really know, although we might suspect, what is really wrong. When we get more evidence of what the problem is, we might get confused about what to do. Our **Adolescent Codependent Survival Behavior** might then go to *caretaking,* like trying to be a better student, son, or daughter. Many of us choose alcohol and drug use. After all, our parents have shown us that this is the way *they* handle stress—which in itself is stressful to us.

*Our codependent survival behaviors get more intense and we develop more of them as time goes on.* This makes it much harder for a person to change as they get older. We get more defensive when confronted about our survival behavior. We deny the problem more and more. And we believe that one—or a combination of these behaviors—will somehow help us feel better. When one doesn't work, we go to another. We can eventually develop numerous self-destructive *compulsive disorders.*

The reason our survival behavior becomes more intense is that the behavior seems to give us relief. But eventually, the relief doesn't come. For example, let's again use the **Event** of *family member develops alcohol & drug abuse problems.* We might begin with the **Adolescent Codependent Survival Behavior** of *rebelling*—fighting and arguing with our parents. When they begin to get the upper hand, we might then use *alcohol & drugs* to get some relief or to get back at them. When our use starts causing problems, we might get *depressed.* We could easily continue to use drugs at this point to medicate the depressed feelings. This pattern often continues until one ore more *compulsive/addictive* problems are happening at the same time. It's not surprising that many of us wind up suffering from problems like chemical dependency, anorexia/bulimia, and depression—all at the same time. Professionals call this a *dual disorder.* It's sad that we have developed these types of problems to escape other problems that weren't ours to begin with. As unfair as it may seem, these problems are ours—and we can learn to deal with them.

*Compulsive/Addictive survival behaviors we carry into adulthood become the events that start the entire process all over again.* These behaviors are the most difficult to deal with and thus repeat themselves over and over. The reason is simple: they take on a life of their own. We may have used alcohol, drugs, food, and sex at an early age to smother the pain of stressful events in our life. But after a while we do these things just because we are hooked on the high they give us. Many, like myself, continue these behaviors into their adulthood and begin the process all over again. We are now doing the survival behavior not because we need to but because we are dependent or addicted to it.

*We will never rid ourselves of the pain of our codependency if we're addicted to escaping it.* If we're stuck in one or a number of these survival behaviors, we'll always be running from the pain.

The feelings are still there because we haven't yet faced them. We may have smothered them for a while with alcohol, drugs, and food, but it's only temporary. We need to do an about face and look at the events that are causing these feelings. As unfair as all this may be, it's our reality. It's what is honestly happening or has happened to us. Look at the chart below. Notice the direction of how things happen.

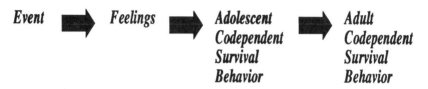

You have already begun disrupting this crippling pattern. You have done this by reading the information in this book. You are beginning to face your codependency. Already, the pattern looks like this:

Facing your codependency does not mean that all the problems are solved. This takes time and work in recovery. You'll learn more about recovery in the next chapter.

# Major Compulsive/Addictive Problems

We can get compulsive about and addicted to almost anything. Some people get addicted to things like reading books, exercising, work, shopping, computers, and music. These things distract us from facing our codependency but are not as destructive as being addicted to chemicals, food, sex, gambling, and criminal behavior. These are the ones we're most likely to get stuck in, the ones that take on a life of their own.

### •*Chemical dependency*

Chemical dependency has to do with mood-altering drugs. Alcohol is the most abused drug, for two reasons. First, it's the easiest and fastest way to smother bad feelings and feel good at the same time. Secondly, society gives us permission to use it. Many of our parents would rather have us use alcohol than other drugs. They don't realize that alcohol is the most destructive drug of all. Alcohol began my chemical dependency. I used it with all the other drugs I took. When I couldn't find other drugs, alcohol was always there.

Here are the three major problems of being dependent on chemicals:

> 1) Chemicals fool us. For a while, they seem to help us. But then they turn on us. They end up causing even more problems and pain.

> 2) Chemicals keep us stuck. We can't grow. All our energy is devoted to maintaining our dependency— searching for ways to get high, and spending all our money to get high.

3) Most importantly, chemicals stop us from being free. They prevent us from being who we are and who we want to be, and keep us chained to the pain of our codependency.

### •*Food*

Eating food can become a compulsion. In time, it can become an addiction. Food seems to fill the emptiness we feel from being abandoned or alone. It can make us feel good when we feel bad. It

can make us feel in control when everything around us is out of control. It can give us a rush just thinking about our next food fix. The problem is, most of us don't want to get fat.

Some of us eat, then diet or exercise compulsively. We may begin a pattern of stuffing down large quantities of food (a food binge) and then deliberately forcing ourselves to throw it up *(purging)*. This unhealthy pattern is called *bulimia*. It is an *eating disorder.*

We might stop eating completely, or eat very little. We may use speed regularly for energy. When we look at ourselves in the mirror, we see fat when we actually may be skin and bones. This eating disorder is called *anorexia.*

Some important facts about eating disorders:

•They can often become life-threatening, cause severe medical problems, and lead to suicide.

•They can destroy our self-esteem; we can begin to hate ourselves and how we look.

•They can keep us stuck, make us unable to face our codependency and free us from the pain.

### •*Sex*

Sex is a normal human function and emotional drive. When we're young, sex is a strange but exciting discovery. Our first sexual experience can be the most exciting high we have ever had—or an incredible low if initiated through some form of abuse such as *rape* or *incest*. How we feel and ultimately react to these early experiences depends on what we have learned about sex from family, society, and peers. Our reactions can lead to compulsive and addictive sexual behavior.

Here is a situation that can bring about addictive sexual behavior: being raised in a family that doesn't make us feel loved and worthwhile. In this situation, we experience many negative feelings. Let's say we have not yet experimented with alcohol or drugs, but we have had our first sexual experience. It can be like having our first drink of alcohol or hit off a joint. It makes us feel good. High. As with alcohol and drugs, we can rapidly become preoccupied with repeating this high over and over. As with alcohol and drugs, we can eventually become addicted to sex.

It's normal, at first, to be preoccupied with sex. But our preoccupation can also become abnormal. Here are a few things to watch out for:

•Our friends tell us we are going "overboard" on sex.

•We already got in trouble over something involving sex (exposing ourselves, date rape).

•We have a bad reputation because of our sexual adventures.

•We begin to lose close friends because they don't like our attitude and behavior regarding sex.

Another situation that can bring about compulsive/addictive sexual behavior is when we have been or are being raised in a sexually exploitative environment. This means we have been sexually abused by adults (rape, incest, and when our parents openly display their sexual activities in front of us). Sexual abuse fools us into believing that love is sex and sex is love. We then begin a pattern of seeking relationships that are focused on sex. We get attracted to people who are openly sexual and seductive. The problem is, we never find the love we want, and we keep searching through the only means we have learned. Eventually, we become addicted to relationships and sex.

A pattern of compulsive sexual behavior may develop from a *sexually repressive environment*. This is actually the opposite of the exploitative environment. Sex is talked about as being "bad" and "immoral." A person feels ashamed to even *think* about sex. This often happens in families that are religiously strict. When we have been told all of our young lives that we'll go to hell if we think about or act out our human sexuality, we're put in a real bind. We all think sexual thoughts from time to time. But when we're told it's not good, we feel flawed. This is the *shame* we talked about earlier. Some of us stay stuck in our shame while others begin acting out against it. Those of us who act out can become extremely rebellious. What better way to get mom and dad upset than to be openly sexual?

It's normal to go through some rebelliousness as we grow into adulthood. But if we rebel using sex, we can very easily turn it into a compulsive/addictive problem.

Here is a summary of compulsive/addictive sexual behavior:

•Like chemicals and food, it does not resolve the
pain of our codependency.

•It is another problem that can take on a life of its
own which we can get stuck in, and prevent
us from experiencing real freedom.

•Besides causing unwanted pregnancies, it can ex-
pose us to *AIDS* and *venereal diseases*.

We can fight these problems by learning about our sexuality.
It's OK to learn about sex. We can even learn to rebel by seeking
out information about unhealthy sexual behavior. You'll learn
more about where to get this information in the *Resources for Recovery* chapter of the book.

### •*Gambling*
Gambling is becoming a major problem for young people today.
Lotteries and pull-tabs are everywhere. Society is telling us it is OK
to gamble. And advertisements bombard us with messages like
*Give it a try—you might become rich!* The reality is, we have a better
chance of becoming addicted than winning the jackpot.

The act of betting gives some people an adrenaline high. Very
early in our life, this high intensifies. We can easily get hooked on
it. If we are in a poverty situation, we can also get hooked on the idea
of striking it rich. We think the next lottery ticket or next bet will
be the way out of the poor house.

### •*Criminal behavior*
Many young people and adults don't look at criminal behavior
as a compulsive/addictive problem. I do. Many young people who
are into stealing, drug dealing, and violent behavior have told me
about the high they get when doing or preparing to do these things.
One young man once told me, "You don't know how hard it is to stop
this. It's like an addiction." He was talking about violent behavior.
He is now serving time for murder. Many times, this young man
spoke with pride about how his relatives engaged in violent behavior. Then it was passed on to him.

I believed that young man back then, but I could do nothing to
help him. The pain of his past—physical abuse, parental alcoholism, and neglect—was too much for him to face. Like many other

youths, he did not believe there were people who could and would help him (Caring Youth workers, social workers, teachers, ministers—even cops). We don't trust these people because they are adults. That puts us in a bind. We can learn to get out of it, though. We can risk trusting an adult.


## How To Figure Out Our Own Codependency

Before we go on to the next chapter on *Recovery,* we have to figure out what we need to recover from. We need to figure out what our individual codependency is and what it looks like. We need to figure out where our bad feelings have come from. And we need to figure out if these things are still happening, and what we can do about them. I will share with you what my codependency looks like. Then I will suggest an activity for you so you can do the same.

Up till now, we have talked mostly about the *problem.* We're now ready to talk about what we can *do* about the problem—the *solution.* We can find the solution in *Recovery*—which is already happening. There are a number of stages of recovery which I will explain in the next chapter.

The *Codependency Worksheet* on the following pages is a process you can use to figure out your codependency. The information is arranged into several columns to show how codependency develops throughout a lifetime. The chapter will end with a suggested activity for us to fill in. Not only is this a way to figure out our codependency, it also offers us a guide for recovery.

# Codependency Worksheet

| | *Not* in Recovery at Age 16 | Adolescent in Recovery | Adult *not* in Recovery | Adult in Recovery |
|---|---|---|---|---|
| **Events** | •Physical/verbal abuse<br>•Father affected by alcohol abuse.<br>•Family secret maintained by family roles. | •Ask for help to deal with abuse.<br>•Learn about how families operate & learn detachment.<br>•With support, bring family secrets into the open. | •Self-abusive; shame.<br>•Denial; self-blaming; confused.<br>•Act out or pass on secrets for our children to act out; possibly both. | •Self-loving; free of shame.<br>•Understand how problems were passed on; forgiveness.<br>•Ability to stop the process of passing on hidden problems to our children. |
| **Roles** | •Acted out scapegoat role to the fullest. Extreme rebel. Kicked out of school. | •Realize we're not the problem. Learn to use "rebel" energy in positive ways. Stay in school. | •Always angry. Blaming everyone for my problems. Acting out against authority. Unable to compromise. | •Take responsibility for my own behavior. Use my rebel behavior for constructive purposes. Better able to accept compromise. |
| **False and Confusing Messages** | •I'm no good.<br>•I'm not lovable.<br>•I'm defective.<br>•Don't try to succeed.<br>•The odds are against you.<br>•Young people are not trustworthy.<br>•I'm a troublemaker.<br>•It's OK to do alcohol and drugs. | •Learn the use of affirmations. Realize we have a choice in how we look at ourselves. Understand that all those messages are not true. Believe that we are OK, capable of doing anything that we work hard for. Have the intelligence and courage to stay away from drugs. | •I'm no good.<br>•I'm not lovable.<br>•I'm defective.<br>•Don't try to succeed.<br>•The odds are against you.<br>•Young people are not to be trusted.<br>•Young people are troublemakers.<br>•Hang out with users for peer acceptance. | •Learn the use of affirmations.<br>•Realize I have a choice in how I look at myself.<br>•Reject all messages of shame.<br>•Belief that I'm OK just the way I am.<br>•Not only can I dream, I can pursue and achieve success.<br>•Believe that I deserve success.<br>•Accept our children as they are.<br>•Believe in our children, and they will believe in us. |
| **Feelings** | •Hurt<br>•Sad<br>•Angry<br>•Abandoned<br>•Shame<br>•Confused<br>•Guilty<br>•Afraid<br>•Rejected<br>•Unloved<br>•Depressed<br>•Hopeless<br>•Mistrust | • Our negative feelings will change when we use our affirmations, face our codependency, and work hard on our recovery program. Our feelings will no longer control us. We will become happy, joyous, and free. | •Hurt<br>•Sad<br>•Rageful<br>•Shamed<br>•Fearful<br>•Arrogant<br>•Judgmental<br>•Flawed<br>•Fatalistic (nothing will ever work out). | • Our negative feelings will change when we use our affirmations, face our codependency, and work hard on our recovery program. Our feelings will no longer control us. We will become happy, joyous, and free. |

# Codependency Worksheet

| | *Not* in Recovery at Age 16 | Adolescent in Recovery | Adult *not* in Recovery | Adult in Recovery |
|---|---|---|---|---|
| *Codependent Survival Behavior* | •Manipulating, lying, arguing with father for attention. Breaking rules to see what parents will do—and to find out if they love me enough to set limits. Skipping school to see if they will discipline me. Numerous girlfriends to make me feel worthwhile. Rejected the idea of a higher power because I felt God had let me down. | •Realized how lying and manipulating kept me away from the love I was seeking (giving my parents more reason to mistrust and reject me). Realized that I needed limits to feel loved and worthwhile (and stopped resisting the set limits). If my parents didn't set them (which they didn't), I would have set them myself. I would have sought love and acceptance from a 12-Step or other support groups. I would have searched for an understanding of spirituality. | •Became more adept at manipulating. Kept looking for reasons to blame others—especially my father. When confronted about my behavior, I would use anger to push people away. Remained lonely and unavailable for a healthy relationship. Felt like a victim—totally powerless to improve my situation. Became severely depressed. Survival behavior turned compulsive and eventually addictive. Chronic alcoholism. Without realizing it, I passed on many of these behaviors to my children. | •Have no need to lie and manipulate because I have learned to accept and love myself. I now own my mistakes. I continue to learn about myself and grow through reading and involvement in 12-Step programs. I risk being involved in close friendships with the opposite sex because I feel worthwhile, deserving of love and care. I accept there is a higher power that helps me when I ask. I accept that I can't handle all my problems, that I can ask for help. Continue to resist beating myself up when I make a mistake. I have learned to accept and love my family as they are. |
| *Compulsive/Addictive Survival Behaviors* | •Chemical dependency. Life completely controlled by my preoccupation with drugs and alcohol. | •Sought to receive treatment for my addiction. Learned about my codependency. Faced my codependency instead of developing another compulsive behavior to escape it. Realized that to be truly happy and free, I needed a healthy support system. I would search out a young people's A.A. group and use the groups at my school. Sought out a CoDA-Teen group, Young A.C.A. | •Chronic alcoholism. Got arrested. Numerous stays in the hospital. Lost jobs. Body began to fall apart. Self-hatred and depression. Defensive, intimidated behavior when confronted about problems. Complete denial. Passed it on to one of my children. | •Recovering in A.A. for the past 14 years. Let down my wall of mistrust and listened to people who could help me. Discovered that working on my codependency was the secret to preventing relapse into my addiction. It also offered me true peace and joy. My children no longer have to suffer from my addiction. Involvement in Al-Anon and Codependents Anonymous. |

68

## Suggested Activity:

Do the best you can when responding to the questions below. This will help you see what your individual codependency looks like. Remember, the information in the previous worksheet shows what *my* codependency looks like. Yours may look much different. Don't let all the questions overwhelm you. Take your time. You may want to go back and re-read some of the information. Or you may just want to think about it a while. That's OK. Do it when you're ready. You'll find that once you do, it will be worth it.

1) What **Events** have or are affecting you? (It's OK to list those I have not mentioned, things like divorce or mental illness of a family member. Include *family secrets* whenever they become the **Events** that cause problems.)

_____

_____

_____

_____

_____

_____

_____

_____

2) What **Role** do you see yourself playing most often?
(Make up your own labels like *burnout* or *little princess* or
*little mother*.) If you're not sure which role you play most
often, list all the ones related to you.

_____

_____

_____

_____

_____

_____

3) List the **Feelings** you experience most often.

_____

_____

_____

_____

_____

_____

_____

4) List the **Codependent Survival Behaviors** you have or are using (make up your own if you have to).

_____

_____

_____

_____

_____

_____

5) List any **Compulsive/Addictive Survival Behaviors** you have used to escape the pain of your codependency.

_____

_____

_____

_____

_____

_____

_____

_____

*What's Wrong With Me?*

Chapter Six

# *Recovery*

The word *recovery* is usually associated with doctors and hospitals. A person who has a medical problem or injury goes to the doctor or hospital to relieve the pain, and to fix the problem so the pain doesn't return. The person who has a medical problem like the flu is said to be sick. If this person follows the prescription given by the doctor, eventually they will get well. The person who is injured is just that—injured. If you had a close friend who was in a car accident, you wouldn't tell your other friends that this person is sick. You would say your friend was injured.

How we go about recovering from codependency is similar to the example of being injured in a car accident. We have been or are being emotionally injured and bruised by events we neither asked for or deserve. And like an accident victim, we need a self-care plan to relieve the pain. It's important to understand that having painful codependency issues does not mean we are sick. We have been injured. We need and deserve immediate attention. Our self-care plan is called a *recovery program*. The first stage of this program is *awareness*.

## Stage I—*Awareness*

Before we can relieve the pain of our codependency and attend to our injuries, we have to admit to being injured. This brings up the first obstacle both young people and adults need to overcome: *denial*.

Young people overcome this obstacle much faster than adults. Adults (including our parents) didn't have information about codependency when they were young. The events that brought about their pain (the original injuries) were left unattended for years. I have noticed that many adults developed chronic (constant) stress-related disorders like depression, or compulsive/addictive problems in an attempt to escape the pain of being injured. Then they were fooled into believing that if they just dealt with their depression by taking pills or their alcoholism by going to treatment, their pain would go away. It usually didn't. Nothing was done about their codependency.

It's unfortunate that many adults in recovery still find themselves relapsing into their old stress disorders, compulsive behaviors, or addictions. I say unfortunate because it isn't their fault. It's also unfair that they still have to keep experiencing the pain of their codependency. For whatever reason, many haven't been able to face it yet.

I developed a pattern like this as an adult recovering from alcoholism and drug addiction. I would overwork, become overwhelmed by it all, then get depressed. I would then work even harder to get myself out of my depression. Eventually this pattern burned me out emotionally and left me feeling incomplete, unrewarded for my work, angry, lonely, and extremely sad. After nine years of this pattern, I finally faced my codependency—admitting that I had been affected in painful ways by events in my life. That was five years ago. I have been working a recovery program for my codependency as well as a program for my addictions ever since.

For young people entering recovery, there's good news: we're better equipped to break through denial because we have the information earlier in our life, and because we haven't had all those years to allow our injuries to go unattended. We also have a chance to break the cycle of passing on problems. When we become parents, we can pass on our recovery to our children. We do this by staying in recovery.

Adults don't have a problem that young people face when entering recovery. Most adults no longer live in the environments where they were injured. For example, they no longer have to live with an abusive or alcoholic parent. Young people are not so fortunate. We have to live and do our best to survive in these types of environments.

This obstacle is not impossible for young people to overcome. When we're given information that will help us overcome our obstacles, we begin to trust that there are other healthier ways to survive our emotional injuries. We are also courageous enough to try them once our immediate needs are taken care of and we understand what these other ways are and how they work. We'll learn more about these things as we go through the remaining stages of recovery.

If we have admitted to ourselves that we have been affected in painful ways by events in our lives, we are facing our codependency. We're ready for the next stage of recovery.


# Stage II—*Bandaging Our Wounds and Regaining Our Strength*

Most of us have been injured in ways that have left us feeling powerless over our situation. We've been bombarded over and over with false messages from our not-so-perfect families—leaving many of us feeling hopelessly flawed. We never have been able to develop a strong liking of ourselves or a positive self-worth. If we add the false and confusing messages from society about young people, we are left feeling depressed, unloved, and hopeless about our future.

For those of us in situations involving physical or sexual abuse, there may be a need to build up our strength or self-worth before we take action and get out. For those who are ready to get out, there are shelters and programs to help you. I will give more information about them later in the *Resources for Recovery* chapter.

### •*Affirmations*
The word *affirm* means *to state positively.* An *affirmation* is *a positive statement about ourselves.* Affirmations are tools to help build our strength or self-worth. When we use affirmations, we tell the truth about ourselves in order to fight off the false messages or lies we have been forced to buy into.

*Affirmations* are the instruments we use to bandage our wounds and regain our strength. These include the *affirmation of our rights* and *affirming ourselves.*

If you are confused about what the truth really is, it's understandable. The following information will help you to straighten things out.

### •*Affirming our rights*

We all have God-given rights, no matter what our age. The only problem is, we've been told over and over that we don't. The rights listed below do not have to be earned. We don't have to do anything to get them. They are our rights just because we have been born into this world. *This is the way it was meant to be.* I encourage you to copy the following bill of rights and post them wherever you feel necessary.

## Young People's Bill of Rights

1) We have the right not to be abused in any way—physically, sexually, emotionally, verbally, or spiritually.

2) We have the right to have our ideas and opinions taken seriously.

3) We have the right to have feelings of every kind which should not be discounted or put down. (We are only responsible for how we act out our feelings.)

4) We have the right to food and shelter.

5) We have the right to be emotionally cared for—to feel safe, secure, worthwhile, and loved.

6) We have the right to experience our teenage years, and not have to become an adult before our time.

7) We have the right to a quality education and adequate healthcare no matter what our financial situation (rich or poor).

8) We have the right to have limits set on our behavior—especially by our parents. (This shows that people care about us).

9) We have the right to mess up sometimes (that's how we learn) and be given consequences that do not punish us or put us down. (These consequences should be designed in such a way as to help us learn from our mistakes.)

10) We have the right to pursue an understanding of the spiritual/religious part of life. (This helps us answer questions like: What is the meaning of life? Why am I here? Is there really a heaven and a hell? Is there a God?)

These are our absolute rights. Adults, including our parents, also have these rights, although they may not have been aware of them when they were young. That's the problem. If they weren't aware of their rights, how could they pass them on to us? Well, now *we* know. Someday, we can pass them onto our children.

## •*Affirming ourselves*
To affirm ourselves as individuals, we need to understand and accept the following:

1) No two people are exactly alike. We can be who we want to be.

2) Nobody is perfect. We all deserve respect for being individuals regardless of how we look or think.

3) Each of us was born with a purpose in mind—a good purpose, a reason to be here. Even if we're faced with things like the loss of a leg or arm, muscular dystrophy, or mental illness, we still have a purpose.

4) The more we affirm ourselves—accepting ourselves unconditionally (we're OK no matter what)—the more we will see what our purpose is. We will discover that one of our primary purposes in life is to enjoy real happiness and freedom.

### •How to develop affirmations

There are a number of ways people in recovery develop and use affirmations, but they all begin the same way: by figuring out what negative messages are affecting them. The process that worked well for me was described in the *Suggested Activity* at the end of Chapter Four (listing negative messages from family, friends, and society).

Using the list of negative messages, we can now make up positive messages. Here are a few examples from my list:

| Negative Messages | Affirmation |
|---|---|
| •I'm not important. | •I am just as important as everyone else. |
| •I'll never achieve anything worthwhile in my life. | •I can achieve anything I set my mind to. |
| •I'm flawed. | •I'm OK just the way I am. |
| •I'm stupid. | •I'm intelligent. |
| •Life is a "bitch." | •Life is an exciting challenge. |
| •I'm a bad person if I make a mistake. | •We all make mistakes; it's OK, I'm OK. |

It's necessary to keep our affirmations as short and positive as possible. If our negative message is I'm not OK and we develop an affirmation that says *I think I'm OK,* we're telling ourselves that we are not really sure. We really believe we are *not* OK. This is what we are trying to change.

We must "act as if" we believe the affirmation, even if we do not. In time, acting "as if" becomes "believing." We do this by developing strong affirmations and using them often. Then we will have gained the strength to help us lead happy, free, and healthy lives.

### •*How to use affirmations*

Whenever I'm late for work, this negative message pops into my head: *It's not OK to make a mistake.* Aware that this is a false message, I immediately fight it by thinking: *We all make mistakes; it's OK, I'm OK.* I will then shorten the affirmation and say over and over to myself: *It's OK to make mistakes.* This doesn't mean that I'm OK with being late for work. I've just admitted that it was a mistake, it's OK to make mistakes, and that I won't be late the next day. By doing this, I won't harm myself by putting myself down and feeling bad.

We can use this method anytime, in any situation. The more we repeat the affirmation, the stronger it gets.

Here's a personal formula I use: For every negative message that pops into my head, I will use an affirmation 10 times.

Here's another: Write down affirmations on pieces of paper and post them on your bedroom mirror, the refrigerator, inside your school locker, and in your notebooks. This serves the same purpose as repeating them over and over because you will be constantly reading them throughout the day.

Sometimes it may be easier to begin with affirmations that have already been developed for us. You can find these in recovery books and hand-outs from 12-Step meetings.

On the following page is a list of affirmations used in a 12-Step program called CoDA-Teen. CoDA-Teen is a program that uses Alcoholics Anonymous (A.A.) principles to deal with teenage codependency issues. Involvement in this and other programs like A.C.A., Al-Ateen, school support programs, and self-esteem groups is the most effective way to use our affirmations. In these support programs, we tell the truth (affirm) to each other. We don't feel alone with our problems. Everybody is in the same boat. If we're not feeling OK about ourselves or we're having problems, we go to one of these group meetings and get the support we need. We get affirmations given to us by the members of the group. We hear things like "It will be OK" and "You're OK." When we combine group involvement with the other methods I described, we get a strong program that gives us real power to believe in ourselves.

### •Other ways to understand and use affirmations

—*Be inventive.* Sometimes when I'm feeling down, I wear bright clothing. My favorite color is yellow, so I will wear a lot of yellow and buy yellow colored items that I can keep around me. Use your imagination and develop your own ideas.

—*Hang around with upbeat and positive people.* This includes friends and adults. Remember early in the book when I talked about two caring teachers who tried to tell me I was OK? If it weren't for them, I wouldn't have had the small flame of self-worth that burned in me during my many dark years. Not all teachers are as caring and supportive, but many are. And for each of us, there is someone who is trying to convince us that we are OK. Listen to them. Talk with them. Let them know what is going on in your life. They can be a life raft for us when we are in a sea of chaos.

—*Take action to affirm your rights.* We've talked about the messages from society that put young people down. Well, we can do something to fight back. More and more, I see youth organizations popping up. They have names like *Neighborhood Youth*

## CoDA-TEEN Affirmations*

• Today I love and accept myself.

• Today I accept my feelings.

• Today I share all my feelings appropriately.

• Today I am allowed to make mistakes.

• Today I like who I am.

• Today I accept who I am.

• Today I am enough.

• Today I accept who you are.

• Today I will not criticize myself or others.

• Today I love and accept myself and others.

• Today I let others be.

• Today I trust my Higher Power.

• Today I am honest with myself and with others.

• Today I forgive myself.

• Today I treat myself with care and gentleness.

• Today I ask my Higher Power for guidance.

• Today I am not my fault or yours.

• Today I have the right to protect my thoughts and feelings.

• Today I am precious and unrepeatable.

• Today I am my own best friend.

• Today I make healthy choices that nurture myself and my recovery.

• Today I am happy to live in *my* body.

• Today I am beautiful inside and out.

• Today I feel part of .....

*Council, Youth in Action,* and *Youth for a Better Community.* Involvement in these organizations gives us the opportunity to show society that we are not what they say, but rather, intelligent, caring, talented people who are proud to be young. We realize that we are the country's future, and we take this responsibility seriously.

## Stage III—*Detachment (Our Healing Begins)*

*Detachment* is the process of breaking away. It is a normal and healthy process. It means *growing* from being dependent on our parents to becoming happy, healthy, and independent young adults. Learning and practicing this process is the key to dealing with our painful codependency issues. Many adults I know who are working on their codependency wish they would have learned and practiced detachment early in their lives. But they were stuck into reacting with codependent survival behaviors, unable to break away from the painful events and the people involved in them (usually their parents). This, they discovered, is what *messed up* their normal development into happy, healthy adults. What we need to learn is healthy detachment from the people (usually *our* parents) and events that *we* are reacting to so we don't repeat the same pattern.

Here's an example of how and when we can practice healthy detachment:

When we're faced with a painful situation (for example, our parents drinking), we come to this conclusion: "Though I wish my parents wouldn't drink, I'm powerless over what they do. I know this because I have tried over and over to get them to stop. I can see now that most of my pain comes from trying to survive or change the situation." We then choose to affirm our rights by saying, "I do not deserve this pain, it's their problem and not mine, and I've got the strength and self-worth to *let it go*." We are no longer reacting to the problem, but acting—acting in our best interest. We no longer use the unhealthy learned survival behavior. We use a new and healthy survival behavior—*detachment*.

Detachment can be difficult to understand. Some people think detachment means to disown or reject a loved one. This isn't true. While detaching, we also practice acceptance. We learn to accept that we can't change or control other people—only ourselves—and that people like our parents may be doing things that have or are affecting us. Still, they are people we care about. We *can* love and hate at the same time. We *love* the people, but we *hate* what they have done or are doing. That's what healthy detachment is all about—separating people from their behavior.

In time, we will understand detachment more clearly. The hardest part is learning when to use it. That's why we need to practice it throughout our recovery. In all the self-help 12-Step programs I know of, *detachment* and *letting go* are common topics of discussion. We remind and support each other to detach and let go of problems that are causing us pain. Involvement in these programs is the most effective way to further understand what detachment is and when we use it.

## Stage IV—*Action, Change, Freedom*

Some of us will do well just by getting involved in a 12-Step program. Others may have to get special help for problems such as chemical dependency or eating disorders before they enter a 12-Step program. Still others may need help for other problems after being involved in a 12-Step program. It depends on the individual circumstances. In any case, involvement in a 12-Step program is always a good first step.

There is another step that should be taken at the beginning. We need to look after the most immediate issues causing us the most pain or potential harm. This includes lack of food, shelter, or medical care, and living in abusive situations. Society has laws to help us will all these problems. All we need to do is ask for help.

## Essential Steps For A Successful Recovery

**1.** *Seek support*—No matter how we begin our recovery, we can't do it alone. Join a 12-Step program. Hang around positive people. Talk with close friends, supportive teachers or counselors at school, a minister you trust, or call one of the hot lines established to help us talk over our problems. (You can find these telephone numbers in the next chapter).

**2.** *Get help for compulsive/addictive problems*—This can simply mean involvement in a 12-Step program, or it may mean getting help at a counseling center or hospital treatment program. We can't get at the source of our pain when we are addicted to trying to escape it.

**3.** *Accept that recovery is a process that takes time*—If we don't give up, we will be successful. We may go backwards at times, but if we stick with it, it will eventually happen. The more we accept this, the faster our recovery will happen.

Although it may seem natural to go right into using what we have learned, it isn't that easy. This stage is where we make a decision to actually *change*—do things differently. Even though change is healthy, it usually makes us feel strange. It is the fear of being vulnerable—leaving ourselves open to the pain we have tried so hard to avoid. This fear is experienced by everyone facing change.

Because change is so scary, it doesn't happen overnight. It takes time, patience, and, most importantly, supportive people in our lives who don't push us. These people need to be like us. They need to be in recovery. They realize we're in a scary process because they too are there. They understand how overwhelmed we feel. They can help us through these hard times and give us encouragement to go on in our recovery. They also help us gain courage and power. This in turn gives us faith that we can face the pain of our codependency, work through it, and become free from it.

There are many types of groups that give us support. But the best ones are 12-Step programs. Here's why:

•They don't push us; they let us grow and change at our own pace.

•They accept us just as we are; this is called unconditional acceptance.

•They offer us a *suggested* program to follow; there are no *have to's.*

•They accept us even if we fall back into our old behavior; they don't kick us out or reject us.

•They constantly offer us support and hope.

•They give us role models who have successfully worked through problems that we too are dealing with.

•They emphasize the use of *affirmations* and the practice of *detachment.*

•They can be used for any problem we have.

•They are free; there are no dues or fees.

In the *Resources for Recovery* chapter, I will list the various 12-Step programs available to us, how they can help with specific problems, and how we can get involved with them—one of which is CoDA-Teen.

CoDA-Teen is a program that was developed fairly recently and is just now beginning to take hold throughout the United States. It is a program for young people dealing with painful codependent issues. It is part of the Codependent Anonymous Program CoDA which is for adults. The best way to explain CoDA-Teen is to share their *Welcome* and *Preamble* which they read before every meeting. I also will share the 12-Steps they follow in their program.

# *CoDA-Teen**

## *Preamble*

*CoDA-Teen, part of the Codependents Anonymous family group, is a fellowship of teens whose common problem is an in ability to maintain functional relationships. We share with one another in the hopes of solving our common problems and helping others to recover. The only requirement for membership is a desire for healthy and fulfilling relationships with others and ourselves.*

*We believe codependency is a family issue because it affects all the members emotionally and sometimes physically. Although we cannot change or control our family or others, we can detach from their problems while continuing to love them.*

*Reprinted with permission of Co-Dependents Anonymous, Inc., ISO, Phoenix, AZ Copyright © 1990.

*What's Wrong With Me?*

*CoDA is not allied with any sect, denomination politics, orga-nization, or institution; does not wish to engage in any controversy; neither endorses nor opposes any causes. We rely upon the wisdom, knowledge, Twelve Steps, and Twelve Traditions, as adopted for our purpose from Alcoholics Anonymous, as the principles of our program and guides to living healthy lives. Although separate entities, we should always cooperate with all twelve-step recovery programs.*

*We are always careful to protect each other's anonymity. We are grateful to CoDA-Teen for giving us a wonderful, healthy program to live by and enjoy.*

## Welcome

*We welcome you to the CoDA-Teen group—a program of recovery from codependency where each of us may share our experience, strength, and hope in our efforts to find freedom where there has been bondage and peace where there has been turmoil in our relationships with others and ourselves. Most of us have been searching for ways to overcome the painful trauma of our loneliness and frustration.*

*We attempted to use others—our friends and families, as our sole source of identity, value, and well-being and as a way of trying to restore within us our emotional losses. Our histories may include other powerful addictions which at times we have used to cope with our codependency. We urge you to try our program; CoDA-Teen has helped many of us to find solutions that lead to serenity. Our recovery depends on our own attitudes and as we learn to place our problem in its true perspective, we find it loses its power to dominate our thoughts and our lives.*

*Our thoughts and feelings about ourselves are bound to improve as we apply the CoDA-Teen ideas. Little by little, one day at a time, we are accomplishing this with the Twelve Steps and principles found in CoDA-Teen, along with our slogans and the Serenity Prayer. We have all learned to survive life, but in CoDA-Teen we are learning to live life. No matter how traumatic your past or despairing your present may seem, there is hope for a new day in the program of CoDA-Teen. No longer do you need to rely upon others as a power greater than yourself. May you instead find here a new strength within to be, that which God intended—precious and free!*

## The Twelve Steps of Codependents Anonymous\*

*1. We admitted we were powerless over others—that our lives had become unmanageable.*

*2. Came to believe that a power greater than ourselves could restore us to sanity.*

*3. Made a decision to turn our will and our lives over to the care of God as we understood God.*

\*The Twelve Steps (or Traditions) of Co-Dependents Anonymous are reprinted for adaptions with permission of Alcoholics Anonymous World Services, Inc.

### The 12 Steps of A.A.

1. We admitted we were powerless over alcohol—that our lives had become unmanageable. 2. Came to believe that a Power greater than ourselves could restore us to sanity. 3. Made a decision to turn our will and our lives over to the care of God as we understood Him. 4. Made a searching and fearless moral inventory of ourselves. 5. Admitted to God, to ourselves, and to another human being the exact nature of our wrongs. 6. Were entirely ready to have God remove all these defects of character. 7. Humbly asked Him to remove our shortcomings. 8. Made a list of all persons we had harmed, and became willing to make amends to them all. 9. Made direct amends to such people whenever possible, except when to do so would injure them or others. 10. Continued to take personal inventory and when we were wrong promptly admitted it. 11. Sought through prayer and meditation to improve our conscious contact with God as we understood Him, praying only for the knowledge of His will for us and the power to carry that out. 12. Having had a spiritual awakening as the result of these steps, we tried to carry this message to alcoholics, and to practice these principles in all our affairs.

*4. Made a searching and fearless moral inventory of ourselves.*

*5. Admitted to God, to ourselves, and to another human being the exact nature of our wrongs.*

*6. Were entirely ready to have God remove all these defects of character.*

*7. Humbly asked God to remove our shortcomings.*

*8. Made a list of all persons we had harmed, and became willing to make amends to them all.*

*9. Made direct amends to such people wherever possible, except when to do so would injure them or others.*

*10. Continued to take personal inventory and when we were wrong promptly admitted it.*

*11. Sought through prayer and meditation to improve our conscious contact with God as we understood God, praying only for knowledge of God's will for us and the power to carry that out.*

*12. Having had a spiritual awakening as the result of these steps, we tried to carry this message to other codependents, and to practice these principles in all our affairs.*

I am personally excited about the CoDA-Teen program. Unfortunately, it may not yet be available in your area. If there isn't a CoDA-Teen meeting operating in your region and you are interested in helping develop one, you can contact them at the address below. They will give you a start-up packet and technical assistance on how to set up meetings.

CoDA-Teen
P.O. Box 33577
Phoenix, Arizona 85067-3577
(602) 277-7991

Even if there isn't a CoDA-Teen meeting in your area, there probably is at least one of the following 12-Step programs available to you: Al-Ateen, Al-Anon, Young Peoples A.A., or Families Anonymous.

## Families In Recovery

It can be a real benefit to us if we have another family member in recovery. That gives us someone to talk to who is close to us, and gives us readily available support. But we need to practice detachment so as not to interfere with each others' programs.

It is strange enough to realize we are changing, but to add another family member—perhaps even a parent—into the picture makes it even more strange. If it is a parent, we need to remind ourselves that they did not have all this information about codependency when they were young and might be struggling more than we are. They also might have a very strong recovery program that we can learn from—if we are willing to communicate with them.

The following is an activity I have found to work well for all families who are struggling to communicate with each other. I learned about it while working as a family counselor at a treatment program in Arizona called *Sierra Tucson*.

91

## *Family Meeting**

*(A tool designed to promote meaningful communication within the family, to enable a dysfunctional family to function again.)*

*Goals: 1. To promote self-disclosure.*
*2. To promote the art of listening.*
*3. To promote the family function of nurturing and thereby meeting the basic human needs of being loved and feeling worthwhile within the family unit.*

*Process:*
*1. The selection of a special time agreeable to all family members. The special time will be honored above any other activity or event. It is essential that this special time be honored. Such keeping of the time-out for the family demonstrates the fact that the family members see the family as more important than anything else.*
*2. The family meeting will be held once a week at the agreed upon special time.*
*3. Members of the family will take turns convening the meeting at the agreed upon time.*
*4. The convener will begin the meeting by sharing his or her reality with the other family members. This self-disclosure is designed to include all feelings; for example:*

> *"This is my joy...."*
> *"I feel disappointed when..."*
> *"I feel pain when..."*
> *"I become angry when..."*
> *"I feel guilty for having done..."*

*\*Reprinted with permission from Sierra Tucson.*

*"I feel proud of myself for..."*
*"I become sad when..."*

**It is extremely important that the person sharing only tell of himself or herself.**

*This is not the time to talk about others, nor is it the time to lecture, preach or gripe. No one is allowed to interrupt the one who is disclosing himself or herself. The other family members must listen until it it their turn to share.*

*When the first person is finished with their self-disclosure, the next person begins. This process of sharing continues until all have shared.*

*5. When all family members have shared themselves, a discussion period may be held for points of clarification, so there is no misunderstanding. It is important to keep this time free from advice, argument, and problem-solving. The discussion time is for clarification only.*

### Warning

*The family meeting is not to be used for solving individual problems of family members, nor is the family meeting to become a group process. If therapy is needed, seek help from qualified persons who are not members of the family. Counseling can occur only when the counselor can remain an objective outsider. The family meeting will help a family to function as a nurturing unit if used as directed.*

### Fair Fight Rules

*In case a disagreement or fight should occur, no one is allowed to leave the room until an agreement, satisfactory to all family members, has been reached. The reason for this is to prove that difficulties can be solved by verbal communication.*

*What's Wrong With Me?*

*These rules for fair fighting may be helpful in the development of a meaningful communication:*

*1. Never attack; keep the focus on self-using "I" statements such as "I feel..." "I sense..." "I think..." "I will..."*

*2. Repeat everything we think we hear to the person who said it.*

*3. Take everything that is said seriously*

*4. Determine the direction of all hostility by asking ourselves, "With whom is this person really angry?" [Maybe they're really angry at someone at work or school.]*

*5. Encourage the other to deal with us as one with whom they can share all of their emotions.*

*Fighting is not necessarily bad. If the fighting is fair, communication continues. The real enemy of communication and relating is silence.*

## Guidelines for Functional Families*

*1. Treat your family members with unconditional positive regard.*

*2. Do not assign blame.*

*3. Do not lecture. Instead, share your perceptions and your feelings.*

*\*Reprinted with permission from Sierra Tucson.*

94

*4. Do not judge the perceptions and feelings of others. Allow them without comment.*

*5. Do not keep score. It is not helpful for me to justify my behavior on your past behavior.*

*6. Always differentiate between behavior and being.*

*7. No matter what happens, hang in there. Do not give up.*

## Have Fun Being Young

Up till now, many of us have been too busy reacting to have much fun. Many of us have had to take on responsibilities like playing the parent role because our parents were unable to do it. In the second stage of recovery, we learned that one of our rights was to *be* a teenager. In this stage, we are ready to act on that right. Even if we have real responsibilities like being a young parent, we can have fun and be responsible at the same time.

This is the time we can try out those things we've always wanted to do: skiing, guitar lessons, dating, going to the movies, hanging out with friends, or shopping for clothes. We will be teens only once in our lifetime. We owe it to ourselves not to pass up the experience.

## Suggested Activity:

At the end of Chapter Five, I suggested an activity to figure out our codependency, using the *Codependency Worksheet* on pages 67 and 68. Now we can use this information for a guide to our recovery. Don't worry if you've only got one issue on your list. It's enough to begin.

List each issue from your *Codependency Worksheet* on the next two pages and put down a possible action to deal with those issues. It may help to go back to Chapter Five to see how I completed mine. Use the *Resources for Recovery* on the following pages.

Remember, recovery is a process that takes time—and patience.

| | Issues From Your Codependency Worksheet | Action |
|---|---|---|
| **Events** | | |
| **Roles** | | |
| **False & Confusing Messages** | | |
| **Feelings** | | |

|  | **Issues From Your Codependency Worksheet** | **Action** |
|---|---|---|
| **Compulsive/Addictive Survival Behaviors** | | |
| **Codependent Survival Behavior** | | |

**Chapter Seven**

# *Resources for Recovery*

## Local Resources

•*The Telephone Book*—Using the yellow pages in your phone book is the fastest way to get in touch with a variety of resources in your area. Look under *Alcohol, Human Services,* or *Social Services.* This will give you a list of programs that may fit your particular need. Many larger communities have a Recovery newsletter circulating around the major hospitals which lists several of the 12-Step programs near you.

•*School*—If you are still enrolled in school, use your counselor or a teacher you trust. There are several support-type programs at most schools. If they don't happen to have a program that fits your needs, talk to a school counselor or principal about starting one.

•*Local Welfare Department*—If you are homeless or in a physically or sexually abusive situation, contact your local Child Protection Agency. They are usually listed under *County Offices* in the phone book. If for some reason you can't get in touch with anyone in your area, there are some toll-free 800 numbers listed in the next section.

•*Churches*—If you're not struggling with compulsive religious issues, you may want to talk to a minister at one of the churches in your area. If you have a minister you know and trust, use him or her.

•*Libraries*—There are many books dealing with specific problems in your local library. One book I strongly suggest is *The Recovery Resource Book* by Barbara Yoder (Fireside/Simon and Schuster). It is the most up-to-date book on recovery resources.

## National Resources

### Homelessness, Physical & Sexual Abuse, and Suicide

•Covenant House Nineline: **800-999-9999.** 24-hour toll-free hotline for kids who need help with drug and alcohol problems, suicidal tendencies, and other major concerns. Covenant House, 440 Ninth Ave., New York, NY 10001.

•National Runaway Hotline: **800-231-6946** (In Texas, call: 800-392-3352). 24-hour toll-free hotline for homeless young people looking for moral support and information about food, shelter, medical assistance, counseling, and free transportation home. Will relay messages to families.

•National Victim Center: **800-877-3355.** Links victims with appropriate services. National Victim Center, 307 West 7th St., #1001, Forth Worth, TX 76102.

•Parents Anonymous (PA): **800-421-0353.** National hotline to help parents build relationships with their children. Parents Anonymous, 6733 S. Sepulveda Blvd., Los Angeles, CA 90045.

•Child Help USA: **800-4-A-CHILD.** National child abuse hotline; publishes educational pamphlets. Child Help USA, PO Box 630, Hollywood, CA 90028.

•National Coalition Against Domestic Violence: **800-333-SAFE.** National hotline for battered women; publishes a resource directory. National Coalition Against Domestic Violence, PO Box 15127, Washington, DC 20003.

•Batterers Anonymous (BA): **714-884-6809.** A program of free weekly meetings that helps men understand and stop their abusive behavior. Batterers Anonymous, 1269 North E Street, San Bernardino, CA 92405.

•Incest Survivors Anonymous: **213-428-5599.** A national self-help recovery program for incest victims. Incest Survivors Anonymous, PO Box 5613, Long Beach, CA 90805.

•Survivors of Incest Anonymous (SIA): **301-282-3400.** A national hotline for victims of incest, molestation, pedophilia, and rape. SIA World Service Office, PO Box 21817, Baltimore, MD 21222.

•Parents United: **408-280-5055.** Support groups for dysfunctional families. 200 chapters nationwide. Parents United, PO Box 952, San Jose, CA 95108.

•Sex Addicts Anonymous (SAA): **612-339-0217.** Support groups that emphasize avoiding compulsive and destructive sexual behavior. 300 groups in the U.S. and Canada. SAA, PO Box 3038, Minneapolis, MN 55403.

## Codependency

•Codependents Anonymous (CoDA), includes CoDA-Teen: **602-944-0141.** Support groups for codependent adults and teens. Sponsors over 1,500 meetings throughout the United States, Canada, and seven other countries. Publishes pamphlets, audiocassettes, and a quarterly newsletter. Codependents Anonymous, PO Box 33577, Phoenix, AZ 85067.

•Codependents Anonymous for Helping Professionals (CODAHP): Support groups that deal with codependency in the workplace, workaholism, and job burnout. CODAHP, PO Box 18191, Mesa, AZ 85212.

• Al-Anon; includes Al-Ateen: **800-356-9996** (in New York, call 800-245-4656; in Canada, call 613-722-1830). The world's largest self-help group for families of alcoholics. Al-Anon, PO Box 862, Midtown Station, New York, NY 10018.

•Adult Children of Alcoholics (ACA): **213-534-1815.** Support group for families of alcoholics. Over 1,350 meetings in five countries. Adult Children of Alcoholics, PO Box 3216, 2522 W. Sepulveda Blvd., Suite 200, Torrance, CA 90505.

•Families Anonymous (FA): **818-989-7841.** Support group for families of drug addicts. Meetings in the United States, Canada, Mexico, England, Australia, and India. Publishes books, booklets, and other materials. Families Anonymous, Inc., PO Box 528, Van Nuys, CA 91408.

•Nar-Anon: **213-547-5800.** Support group for families of drug addicts. Meetings throughout the United States and Canada. Publishes a newsletter. Nar-Anon, PO Box 2562, Palos Verdes, CA 90274.

•Gam-Anon: Support group for families of compulsive gamblers. Publishes pamphlets. Gam-Anon International Service Office, PO Box 157, Whitestone, New York, NY 11357.

•O-Anon: Support group for friends and relatives of compulsive eaters. Over 60 meetings nationwide. Publishes a directory. O-Anon, PO Box 4305, San Pedro, CA 90731.

•Fundamentalists Anonymous (FA): **212-696-0420.** Support group for those hurt by the fundamentalist experience. Publishes booklets and offers a telephone support network. Fundamentalists Anonymous, PO Box 20324, Greeley Square Station, New York, NY 10001.

### Alcohol & Other Chemical Addictions
•National Council on Alcoholism (NCA): **800-NCA-CALL.** National hotline for those concerned about their own drinking or

that of a loved one. Publishes literature. National Council on Alcoholism, 12 West 21st Street, New York, NY 10010.

•Alcoholics Anonymous (AA): The world's largest support group for alcoholics. Sponsors young people's meetings, one-fifth of the members are 30 years old or younger, more understanding and acceptable of young alcoholics; publishes materials. Alcoholics Anonymous World Services, PO Box 459, Grand Central Station, New York, NY 10017.

•Student Assistance Programs (SAPs): Exists in thousands of schools throughout the country. Offers a range of services to deal with chemical dependency, suicide, pregnancy, and other teen issues.

•Friday Night Live: **916-445-7456** (California only). Organizes alcohol- and drug-free events for students. Friday Night Live, California Department of Alcohol and Drug Programs, 111 Capitol Mall, Room 223, Sacramento, CA 95814.

### Special Populations

•Institute on Black Chemical Abuse (IBCA): **612-871-7878.** National organization devoted to fighting alcoholism and drug addiction in the African American community. Conducts educational workshops; publishes booklets. IBCA, 2614 Nicollet Ave. S., Minneapolis, MN 55408.

•National Black Alcoholism Council (NBAC): **312-663-5780.** Promotes awareness about alcoholism among African Americans; offers workshops; publishes newsletter. NBAC, 417 South Dearborn St., Suite 1000, Chicago, IL 60605.

•Indian Health Service (IHS): Provides alcoholism and substance abuse programs for Native Americans and Alaskan Natives. Contact the IHS office in your region.

•National Asian Pacific Families Against Substance Abuse (NAPAFASA): **301-530-0945.** National prevention and educational group for Asian Pacific communities in the U.S. NAPAFASA, 6303 Friendship Court, Bethesda, MD 20817.

•National Association of Lesbian and Gay Alcoholism Professionals (NALGAP): **212-713-5074.** Support network for gay and lesbian recovery professionals. NALGAP, 204 West 20th St., New York, NY 10011

•Pride Institute: **800-54-PRIDE** (in Minnesota: 612-934-7554). A treatment center for gays and lesbians. Pride Institute, 14400 Martin Dr., Eden Prairie, MN 55344.

### Street Drugs

•Covenant House Nineline: **800-999-9999.** 24-hour toll-free hotline for kids who need help with drug and alcohol problems, suicidal tendencies, and other major concerns. Covenant House, 440 Ninth Ave., New York, NY 10001.

•National Institute on Drug Abuse (NIDA): **800-662-HELP** (Monday thru Friday, 9 A.M. to 8 P.M.). Toll-free helpline providing drug-related information and help.

•Narcotics Anonymous (NA): **818-780-3951.** Offers meetings for drug abusers. Sponsors 15,000 groups in the United States and Canada and in 41 countries worldwide. Narcotics Anonymous, PO Box 9999, Van Nuys, CA 91409.

### Eating Disorders

•Overeaters Anonymous (OA): **213-542-8386.** Support group for overeaters. 9,000 groups worldwide. Overeaters Anonymous, World Service Office, PO Box 92870, Los Angeles, CA 90009.

•Food Addiction Hotline: **800-USA-0088** (Monday thru Friday—8 A.M. to 8 P.M., Saturday and Sunday—Noon to 4 P.M.). Offers advice and treatment options; helps locate support group meetings.

•Anorexics/Bulimics Anonymous (ABA): Support group for persons suffering from eating disorders. Anorexics/Bulimics Anonymous, PO Box 112214, San Diego, CA 92111.

## Gambling

•Gamblers Anonymous (GA): Support group for those addicted to gambling. 1,000 groups worldwide. Gamblers Anonymous, International Service Office, PO Box 17173, Los Angeles, CA 90017.

•Gam-A-Teen: Support group for teens whose families are affected by gambling. Contact GA, Gam-Anon, or the National Council on Compulsive Gambling for local meetings.

## Nicotine

•Nic-Anon: Support group for families and friends of smokers; helps them deal with codependent issues. Nic-Anon, 511 Sir Francis Drake Blvd., C-170, Greenbrae, CA 94904.

•Smokers Anonymous: **415-922-8575.** National support group for those addicted to nicotine. Smokers Anonymous, 2118 Greenwich St., San Francisco, CA 94123.

*What's Wrong With Me?*

**Epilogue**

# *A Personal Message of Hope*

At this point, I need to say good-bye to you, the reader of this book. But strangely, I find it difficult to do so. My desire to help relieve your suffering by sharing my past pain and hope for recovery has bound us together. I know the reader of this book is suffering the same kind of pain I once did—feeling hurt, sad, and confused, looking for answers as I was when running down the street thinking, "What's wrong with me?" and "How can I fix it?" and wanting so much to be happy and feel loved. I can understand your situation, just as you can understand mine. That's how I know I can help. We're all in the same boat, on the same journey.

Good luck and God bless.

*What's Wrong With Me?*

## About The Author

Lonny Owen is a Certified Senior Alcohol Drug Counselor and Director of the Highland Park Teen Center in Minneapolis, Minnesota, a program for inner-city youth. He has been in the chemical dependency field since 1979, and has counseled chemically dependent adolescents since 1980, working as an aftercare  counselor, a family counselor and consultant, a county AODA coordinator, a substance abuse specialist, a chemical dependency program coordinator, and an outpatient counselor.

Lonny has also specialized in providing innovative codependency programing for adults and youths. He has presented numerous workshops on codependency for professional counselor organizations, schools, and clergy associations, including a 10-week support group workshop co-facilitated with Melody Beattie (*Codependent No More, The Language Of Letting Go*) on advanced recovery issues. Lonny also provides consulting services to inpatient and out-patient chemical dependency and residential programs dealing with youth problems. He has fourteen years of sobriety.

# Notes

_____

_____

_____

_____

_____

_____

_____

_____

_____

_____

_____

_____

_____

_____

_____

_____

_____

_____

# Notes

*What's Wrong With Me?*

**Notes**

_____

_____

_____

_____

_____

_____

_____

_____

_____

_____

_____

_____

_____

_____

_____

_____

_____

_____

_____

# Notes

**Notes**

_____

_____

_____

_____

_____

_____

_____

_____

_____

_____

_____

_____

_____

_____

_____

_____

_____

_____

# Other Books and Publications from

# DEACONESS PRESS

## Books for Teens

•*Little By Little The Pieces Add Up* (Daily readings for teens)
  ISBN: 0-925190-11-X, $7.95
•*Life Is Just A Party: Portrait of a Teenage Partier* (Fiction for teens)  ISBN: 0-925190-05-5, $6.95
•*Taking The First Step: Being Honest with Yourself* (12-Step booklet) ISBN: 0-925190-03-9, $1.75
•*Getting Help, Gaining Hope: The Second and Third Steps for Teens*  ISBN: 0-925190-10-1, $1.75

## Books for Parents

•*Designer Kids—Consumerism and Competition: When is it all too much?* (Parenting) ISBN: 0-925190-12-8, $10.95
•*I've Got It Under Control? A Parent's Guide to the First Step*
  New & Revised—ISBN: 0-925190-18-7, $1.75
•*Working The Program: The Second and Third Steps for Parents*  ISBN: 0-925190-13-6, $1.75
•*Relationships At Risk: Assessing Your Kid's Drug Abuse Potential* (Prevention) ISBN: 0-925190-02-0, $6.95

To order or receive a *free* catalog, write to:

Deaconess Press
2312 S. 6th Street
Minneapolis, MN 55454
or call toll-free:
**1-800-544-8207**